GOD'S BIG PICTURE

VAUGHAN ROBERTS

GOD'S BIG PICTURE

Tracing the story-line
of the Bible

ivp

Inter-Varsity Press

INTER-VARSITY PRESS
38 De Montfort Street, Leicester LE1 7GP, England
Email: ivp@uccf.org.uk
Website: www.ivpbooks.com

First published 2002
Reprinted 2003 (twice), 2004

British Library Cataloguing in Publication Data
A catalogue record for this book is available from the British Library.

ISBN 0–85111–298–6

Set in Dante 10.5 / 13pt
Typeset in Great Britain by CRB Associates, Reepham, Norfolk
Printed and bound in Great Britain by Creative Print & Design
(Wales), Ebbw Vale

Inter-Varsity Press is the publishing division of the Universities and
Colleges Christian Fellowship (formerly the Inter-Varsity Fellowship), a
student movement linking Christian Unions in universities and colleges
throughout Great Britain, and a member movement of the
International Fellowship of Evangelical Students. For more information
about local and national activities write to UCCF, 38 De Montfort Street,
Leicester LE1 7GP, email us at email@uccf.org.uk, or visit the UCCF
website at www.uccf.org.uk.

Contents

To my parents
with much love
and gratitude

Acknowledgments

I am grateful to Clare Heath-Whyte and Matthew Mason for commenting on the manuscript, to Andy Rees and David Heath-Whyte for help with the diagrams, and to Jonty Frith for suggesting the title.

Preface

'Which passages would you choose if you were devising a series of Bible studies on the theme of the temple?'

It was an innocent question from a young man I had just met at a conference for trainee ministers. I was about to start at college. Within two years I would be let loose on a church, and I was far from ready. I had been a committed Christian for six years, but my knowledge of the Bible, especially the Old Testament, was very limited – which explains why my new friend's question unnerved me so much. I had heard of the temple, but I did not really know what its significance was, and had no idea where to look in the Bible to find out more; so I stalled: 'Which passages would *you* choose?'

In the next ten minutes I was taken on a whistle-stop tour of the whole Bible that left my head reeling. We began in the garden of Eden, where Adam and Eve did not need a temple because God's presence was everywhere; and travelled to the new creation, heaven, where once again there is no temple 'because the Lord God Almighty and the Lamb are its temple' (Revelation 21:22). Along the way we made brief stops at the tabernacle in the wilderness; the temple in Jerusalem; the new-temple prophecies of Ezekiel; the Lord Jesus Christ, who 'tabernacled' among us

(John 1:14, literally); and the church ('a holy temple in the Lord', Ephesians 2:21).

I was very impressed. I had already completed a theology degree at university, but it left me unable to find my way around the Bible. There had been detailed analysis of individual books and passages, but no-one had shown me how they fitted together. My friend, however, was able to travel through the Bible with apparent ease. It was as if he was using a map while I was left without any sense of direction. I asked him how he did it. He told me about a book that outlined the main elements in the story of the Bible from beginning to end. It was Graeme Goldsworthy's *Gospel and Kingdom*.[1] I bought it the next day and read it within the week. At last I had the map I needed. I was still very ignorant about much of the Bible, but the framework was in place.

Anyone who has read *Gospel and Kingdom* will see its influence in these pages. This is not an attempt to improve on that book. I adopt largely the same approach, but hope to do so in a slightly less technical way. My aim is to provide all Christians, from the new convert to the mature believer, with an overview of the whole Bible that will help them see how the different parts fit together. I hope the book will be simple without being simplistic. I want to put into the reader's hands the map that I have found so helpful.

A Bible study outline is provided at the end of each chapter (and an extra one in the long chapter 4). These are designed for individual or group use. You will gain more from these studies if you, or the members of your group, read the chapter (or the relevant half of chapter 4) in advance.

I am grateful to Richard Coekin, who first set me on the road, and to Graeme Goldsworthy, whose book gave me the map. This material was originally prepared for talks at St Ebbe's Church, Oxford, Titus Trust Holidays, Spring Harvest Word Alive and the FIEC Caister conference. I have benefited from the teaching of many writers and speakers in this area, including Shaun Atkins, F. F. Bruce, Edmund P. Clowney, Jonathan Fletcher, Ian Garrett,

Phillip Jensen, Walter J. Kaiser, Simon Manchester, Mark Meynell, Alec Motyer, Mike Neville, Alan Purser and Simon Scott. Very few good thoughts are new and I make no apology for standing on the backs of others throughout this book. I forget where I first heard many of these ideas. If you recognize your back, thank you!

Vaughan Roberts

Introduction

The Bible is one book

Ignorance of the Bible

A police inspector went to visit a primary school, where he was asked to take a Scripture class. He began by asking, 'Who knocked down the walls of Jericho?'

There was a long silence as the children shuffled nervously on their seats. Eventually, a little lad put up his hand and said, 'Please sir, my name is Bruce Jones. I don't know who did it but it wasn't me.'

The policeman thought that reply very cheeky, so he reported the incident to the headmaster. After a pause the headmaster replied, 'I know Bruce Jones; he's an honest chap. If he said he didn't do it, then he didn't.'

The inspector was exasperated. The headmaster was either rude or very ignorant. The inspector wrote to the Department of Education to complain, and received this response: 'Dear Sir, We are sorry to hear about the walls of Jericho and that nobody has admitted causing the damage. If you send us an estimate we will see what we can do about the cost.'

It is a silly story and it is probably not true, but it does make a point. A few decades ago everyone would have known about Joshua and the walls of Jericho. A large proportion of children went to Sunday school, and the rest still received a grounding in the main stories of the Bible in class. But those days are gone. I mentioned the prodigal son to an Oxford student recently. He looked blankly at me. The average non-Christian is almost completely ignorant of the contents of the Bible. It remains the world's best-selling book; one and a quarter million copies are sold in the UK alone every year. But although many have a copy on their shelves, very few ever read it.

The knowledge of Christians is often not much better. We all have our favourite passages, but much of Scripture remains uncharted territory, especially the Old Testament. If we are honest, we find it outdated and rather un-Christian at times. What have dietary laws, animal sacrifices and the temple got to do with Jesus Christ? And what about the exodus from Egypt, David and Goliath, and Daniel in the lion's den? They are great stories, but what relevance have they got for us today? I hope this book will answer those questions, or at least give you a framework that will enable you to answer them for yourself. Its aim is to help Christians to find their way around the Bible and to see how it all holds together and points us to Jesus.

A diverse collection of writings

The Bible is a diverse collection of different writings. It contains sixty-six books written by about forty human authors over nearly 2,000 years. It has two main sections (Old Testament and New

History	Poetry	Prophecy
(Genesis to Esther)	(Job to Song of Songs)	(Isaiah to Malachi)

Figure 1. The Old Testament (English Bible)

Testament) written in two main languages (Hebrew and Greek respectively), and includes a mixture of types of literature.

In our English Bibles, the thirty-nine books of the Old Testament are arranged as in Figure 1. This order follows the Greek translation of the Hebrew Bible, the Septuagint, made in the third century BC.

The original Hebrew Bible arranges the books in a different order, listed in Figure 2.

Law	Prophets	Writings
Genesis to Deuteronomy	*Former Prophets* (history books Joshua to 2 Kings) *Latter Prophets* (Isaiah to Malachi)	Psalms, wisdom literature, history of the exile and beyond

Figure 2. The Old Testament (Hebrew Bible)

The New Testament consists of twenty-seven books, all written in the first century AD. The Gospels are four accounts of the birth, life, teaching, death and resurrection of Jesus. Acts, written by Luke as a continuation of his Gospel, records the spread of the good news about Jesus after his ascension into heaven. The Epistles are letters written mainly by those chosen by Christ to be his apostles. The Holy Spirit revealed to them all the truth about Christ so they could teach the full significance of his salvation and its implications. Paul wrote most of the Epistles (Romans to Philemon), but the New Testament also contains letters from Peter, John, James (the brother of Jesus) and Jude. No-one knows who wrote the letter to the Hebrews. That just leaves the last book of the Bible: Revelation. It describes a vision that John was given of spiritual realities normally hidden from view. (See Figure 3.)

Gospels	Matthew, Mark, Luke, John
Acts	Luke's history of the spread of the gospel in the first century
Epistles	Romans to Jude (letters written mostly by the apostle Paul)
Revelation	John's vision from God

Figure 3. The New Testament

One author

Although the Bible contains a great variety of material, written by many human authors over a long period of time, it holds together as a unity. Fundamentally, it is just one book written by one author with one main subject. As those truths underlie everything that is written in the rest of *God's Big Picture*, it is important that we understand them before we continue.

The apostle Paul wrote, 'All scripture is God-breathed' (2 Timothy 3:16). Most of the New Testament had not been written down at that time, so he was referring to what we know as the Old Testament. But the New Testament writers made a similar claim about what they wrote. They were convinced that their teaching was also the very Word of God (e.g. 1 Corinthians 14:37; 1 Thessalonians 2:13; 2 Peter 3:16).

Muslims are taught that Muhammad had no creative role in the production of their holy book. He acted simply as a secretary who wrote down what was dictated to him by Allah via the angel Gabriel. They would be outraged by the suggestion that the Qur'an was in any way a human book. But Christians should have no qualms about accepting that the Bible was written by people. Its books were written by a variety of authors at different times in history and bear the marks of the personalities and eras that produced them. But God ensured by his Spirit that everything they wrote was exactly what he wanted them to write. Just as the

Lord Jesus was both fully human and fully divine, so the Bible is both a human and a divine book. It is God's Word: he is the ultimate author.

One subject

The Bible obviously covers a great deal of ground. But there is one supreme subject that binds it all together: Jesus Christ and the salvation God offers through him. That is true not just of the New Testament but of the Old as well. Jesus, speaking of the Old Testament, said, 'These are the Scriptures that testify about me' (John 5:39). After he had risen from the dead he met two believers on the road to Emmaus and led them in a Bible study. What a privilege for them! 'Beginning with Moses and all the prophets, he explained to them what was said in all the Scriptures concerning himself' (Luke 24:27). A short time later he met with his disciples and said, 'This is what I told you while I was still with you: Everything must be fulfilled that is written about me in the law of Moses, the Prophets and the Psalms' (Luke 24:44). He refers there to the three main divisions of the Hebrew Bible (the Writings were sometimes called 'the Psalms' because the Psalms made up the largest part of them). The apostle Paul also believed that the Old Testament points to Jesus. He spoke of 'the holy Scriptures [the Old Testament] which are able to make you wise for salvation through faith in Christ Jesus' (2 Timothy 3:15).

Many Christians have an idea that God decided to send Jesus to earth only after his first plan had failed; his original idea (Plan A) was to give people an opportunity to become his people by obeying his law. But they failed, so he scratched his head and came up with another idea (Plan B): to save people by grace through the death of Jesus. Nothing could be further from the truth. God had always planned to send Jesus. The whole Bible points to him from beginning to end. In the Old Testament God points forward to him and promises his coming in the future. In the New Testament God proclaims him to be the one who fulfils all those promises (Figure 4).

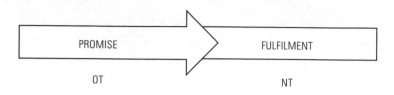

Figure 4. God's plan

Not a book of quotations

The fact that the Bible is one book should have big implications for the way we read it. The way you read a book depends on the kind of book you think it is. So, for example, we do not read a Shakespeare play in the same way as a telephone directory, or a novel in the same way as a book of quotations. I have just opened a book of political quotations at random and read Winston Churchill's comment on Field Marshall Montgomery: 'In defeat unbeatable; in victory unbearable.' The compiler of that book does not expect me to read those words in context. I do not have to read the quotations that appear immediately before and after it. Each saying in the book stands alone.

A novel works very differently. Each sentence is meant to be understood in the light of the whole. Turning to a random page in Agatha Christie's *The Body in the Library* I read, 'Risk everything – that's my motto! Yes, it's a lucky thing for me that somebody strangled that poor kid.' I am left confused. Who is speaking? And who has been strangled? If I am to understand the story, I need to know what happened before and learn what happens afterwards.

It is the same with the Bible. With the exception of some of the Proverbs, the Bible does not contain isolated sayings. I should be wary about dipping into it at random and extracting individual verses without any regard for their context. I am almost bound to misunderstand the Bible if I read it in that way. Each verse needs to be understood in the context of the chapter in which it appears, and each chapter in the light of the book as a whole. And there is a wider context we must consider as well: the whole Bible.

Not a collection of books

I own a collection of Hermann Hesse novels. Each is an individual book that can be read and understood in isolation from the others; they just happen to be bound in the same cover. Many people read the Bible as if it were like that: a collection of independent books that can each be read without reference to the others. That was how I was taught the Bible at university. We looked for the message of Ezekiel, Jonah or John without considering how those biblical books contribute to and fit in with the message of the Bible as a whole. And there was a great division between the Old and New Testaments. I was criticized when I mentioned Jesus in an answer to the question, 'Who is the servant in Isaiah's prophecy?' We were discouraged from reading the Bible as the Bible itself demands to be read: as one book that presents the unfolding story of God's plan to save the world through his Son Jesus. If we want to understand any part of the Bible properly, we must consider where it fits in that great plan and how it contributes to it.

One book

Andy's children are avid readers. He has just bought the latest Agatha Christie novel for Matt. Lizzie announces that she wants to read it too. The bookshop is out of stock and Lizzie will accept no substitute, nor will she wait for her brother to finish it. In desperation, Andy takes the book and tears it in half and gives his children half each. Both are soon very frustrated. Matt discovers that Colonel Bufton-Tufton has been killed with a candlestick in the billiard room, but his part of the book ends before he can find out who committed the crime. Lizzy reads that 'the butler did it', but she has no idea what he did.

No-one would really be so foolish as to divide an Agatha Christie book like that. Both parts must be read together; they do not make sense otherwise. The same is true of the Bible. The Old Testament on its own is an unfinished story; a promise without a fulfilment. We must read on to the New Testament if we want to know what it really means. And the New Testament constantly looks back to the promise it fulfils. We shall not make much sense of it if we are not aware of what has come before. What does it mean that Jesus is the Christ, the Passover lamb, the Son of Abraham and Son of David, the true vine or the good shepherd?[1] The answers are all found in the Old Testament. The Bible must be understood and read as one book with one ultimate author, God, and one ultimate subject, God's plan of salvation through his Son Jesus.

I am told that when SAS soldiers parachute into unknown territory they are trained to pause before moving. They must first get their bearings and only then set out for their destination. That is wise advice for us too as we read the Bible. My aim in this book is to give you an overview of the main storyline of the Bible. It will not make you an expert in all the details of Scripture, but I hope that it will enable you to get your bearings when you land in any part of it. By the end of this book you should have the outline of the Bible's story in your mind so that, whichever part you are reading, you should know where you have come from and where you are heading. That will also help you to discover how each part points to Jesus Christ and the salvation he accomplished.

The kingdom of God

Scholars have debated for years whether or not it is possible to point to a unifying theme that binds the whole Bible together. Many have argued that the search for such a theme is fruitless: it is better just to accept that Scripture contains a number of different threads and then look at them individually without trying to unite them. They warn of the danger of squeezing all parts of the Bible into a mould rather than letting them speak individually in their rich variety. That is an important warning that must be heard. Any unifying theme that is used to help us to see how the Bible fits together must arise out of Scripture itself, rather than being imposed upon it; and it must be broad enough to allow each part to make its own distinct contribution. The theme of the kingdom of God satisfies both requirements.

God's kingdom was the dominant theme in Jesus' teaching. He began his public ministry by proclaiming, 'The time has come . . . The kingdom of God is near' (Mark 1:15). He taught that his mission was to introduce the kingdom in fulfilment of the prophecies of the Old Testament. Although the expression 'kingdom of God' does not appear in the Old Testament, the concept certainly does. Graeme Goldsworthy, in his book *Gospel and Kingdom*, helpfully presents the kingdom as the binding theme of the whole Bible. I am following his lead in this book. This 'kingdom approach' is not the only way of looking at the contents of the Bible. Others, for example, prefer a 'covenantal approach' and take God's covenant to be the centre around which all the elements of Scripture circle. I hope it will become clear that these two approaches are not contradictory. God's covenant promises are kingdom promises.

The kingdom of God:
God's people in God's place under God's rule and blessing

Figure 5. The kingdom of God

Goldsworthy defines the kingdom as 'God's people in God's place under God's rule' (Figure 5).[2] That may sound like an overly simplistic definition for such a significant theme in Scripture, but the simple words contain great depth. God longs for human beings to enjoy an intimate relationship with him in his presence. As he is a perfect, holy God, that is possible only as we submit to his loving rule and do not sin. That is life at its best; life as it was designed to be lived.

To live under God's rule means to enjoy God's blessing; the two go together. That is what we see at the creation in the garden of Eden until the fall. But then human beings disobey God and forgo his blessing. The consequences are devastating not just for humanity but for the whole creation; everything is spoilt. But in his great love God promises to put things right again and re-establish his kingdom on earth. The rest of the Bible tells the story of the fulfilment of that promise: partially in Israel's history in the Old Testament period, and then perfectly through Jesus Christ. So the Bible is about God's plan of salvation: his promise to restore his kingdom, and then the fulfilment of that promise through his Son Jesus.

A Bible overview

When I studied English literature at school I found it a great help to buy a study guide to whichever book I was reading. It would always give a synopsis of the main sections, which summarized a long book in just a page or two. (See Figure 6.) I have divided the Bible into eight sections, which are the main epochs in God's unfolding plan to restore his kingdom. The names I have given these sections provide the chapter headings for the rest of this book. Forgive the alliteration, which has resulted in one or two rather weak headings. I have stuck with it to make it easier for you to remember them.

The Old Testament
    1. The pattern of the kingdom
    2. The perished kingdom
    3. The promised kingdom
    4. The partial kingdom
    5. The prophesied kingdom
The New Testament
    6. The present kingdom
    7. The proclaimed kingdom
    8. The perfected kingdom

Figure 6. An overview of the Bible

The Old Testament

1. *The pattern of the kingdom.* In the Garden of Eden we see the world as God designed it to be. God's people, Adam and Eve, live in God's place, the garden, under his rule as they submit to his word. And to be under God's rule in the Bible is always to enjoy his blessing; it is the best way to live. God's original creation shows us a model of his kingdom as it was meant to be.

2. *The perished kingdom.* Sadly, Adam and Eve think life would be better if they lived independently of God. The results are disastrous. They are no longer God's people. They turn away from him and he responds by turning away from them. They are no longer in God's place; he banishes them from the garden. And they are not under God's rule, so they do not enjoy his blessing. Instead, they face his curse and are under his judgment. The situation is very gloomy. But God, in his great love, is determined to restore his kingdom.

3. *The promised kingdom.* God calls Abraham and makes some unconditional promises to him: through Abraham's descendants he will re-establish his kingdom. They will be his people, living in his land and enjoying his blessing, and through them all peoples on earth will be blessed. That promise is the gospel. It is partially fulfilled in the history of Israel, but is only finally fulfilled through Jesus Christ.

4. *The partial kingdom.* The Bible records how God's promises to Abraham are partially fulfilled in the history of Israel. Through the exodus from Egypt, God makes Abraham's descendants his very own people. At Mount Sinai he gives them his law so that they might live under his rule and enjoy his blessing, as Adam and Eve had done before they sinned. The blessing is marked chiefly by God's presence with his people in the tabernacle. Under Joshua they enter the land and, by the time of Kings David and Solomon, they enjoy peace and prosperity there. That was the high point of the history of Israel. They were God's people in God's place, the land of Canaan, under God's rule and therefore enjoying his blessing. But the promises to Abraham had still not been

completely fulfilled. The problem was sin, the continual disobedience of the people of Israel. That was soon to lead to the dismantling of the partial kingdom as Israel fell apart.

5. *The prophesied kingdom.* After the death of King Solomon civil war broke out and the kingdom of Israel split into two parts: Israel in the north and Judah in the south. Neither was strong. After 200 years of separate existence, the northern kingdom of Israel was destroyed by the Assyrians. The southern kingdom struggled on for another century, but then it too was conquered and its inhabitants were taken into exile in Babylon. During this depressing period in their history God spoke to the people of Israel and Judah through some prophets. He explained that they were being punished for their sin but still offered hope for the future. The prophets pointed forward to a time when God would act decisively through his King, the Messiah, to fulfil all his promises. The people of Judah must have thought that that time had come when they were allowed to return from exile, but God made it clear that the great time of salvation was still in the future. That is where the Old Testament ends: waiting for God's King to appear to introduce his kingdom.

The New Testament

6. *The present kingdom.* Four hundred years passed after the completion of the Old Testament before Jesus began his public ministry with the words, 'The time has come . . . The kingdom of God is near' (Mark 1:15). The waiting was over; God's king had come to establish God's kingdom. His life, teaching and miracles all proved that he was who he said he was: God himself in human form. He had the power to put everything right again, and he chose a very surprising way of doing it: by dying in weakness on a cross. It was by his death that Jesus dealt with the problem of sin and made it possible for human beings to come back into relationship with his Father. The resurrection proved the success of Jesus' rescue mission on the cross and announced that there is hope for our world. Those who trust in Christ can look forward to eternal life with him.

7. *The proclaimed kingdom.* By his death and resurrection Jesus did all that was necessary to put everything right again and completely restore God's kingdom. But he did not finish the job when he was first on earth. He ascended into heaven and made it clear that there would be a delay before he returned. The delay is to enable more people to hear about the good news of Christ so they can put their trust in him and be ready for him when he comes. We live during this period, which the Bible calls 'the last days'. It began on the Day of Pentecost when God sent the Spirit to equip his church to tell the whole world about Christ.

8. *The perfected kingdom.* One day Christ will return. There will be a great division. His enemies will be separated from his presence in hell, but his people will join him in a perfect new creation. Then at last the gospel promises will be completely fulfilled. The book of Revelation describes a fully restored kingdom: God's people, Christians from all nations, in God's place, the new creation (heaven), under God's rule and therefore enjoying his blessing. And nothing can spoil this happy ending. It is no fairy story; they really will all live happily ever after.

The pattern of the kingdom

Genesis 1 – 2, the first two chapters of the Bible, show us God's original, perfect creation. They present us with a vision of how the world is meant to be. I want us to notice four important truths about creation.

1. God is the author of creation

The Bible begins with the declaration, 'In the beginning God created the heavens and the earth' (Genesis 1:1). He alone is eternal. There has never been a time when God, the three in one, was not. Jesus became incarnate, taking on human flesh, only when he was born in the manger in Bethlehem; but that was not the beginning of his existence. God has always been a trinity: Father, Son and Holy Spirit. He existed before anything else came into being. Then he just said the word and the universe came into existence out of nothing. Whether he completed the job in six literal twenty-four-hour days or over a longer period does not really matter (Christian opinions differ over how we should interpret Genesis 1). What is important is the fact that God is the creator of all things.

God the Father took the initiative. Genesis tells us that the Spirit was also involved: 'the Spirit of God was hovering over the waters' (1:2). And the New Testament teaches that Jesus, the Son of God, was his Father's agent in creation: 'Through him all things were made; without him nothing was made that has been made' (John 1:3); 'all things were created by him and for him' (Colossians 1:16).

The Bible stresses that God is pleased with what he has made. After each of his days of creative labour, except the first two, we are told, 'God saw that it was good'; and, when he finished the job (the writer of Genesis comments), 'God saw all that he had made, and it was very good' (1:31).

This attitude to the material world is very different from that of many philosophies and religions, which are really concerned only with the spiritual and the soul. Everything else is regarded, at best, as of secondary importance, and, at worst, as evil. Their understanding of salvation involves the soul being released from the prison of the body to join the non-material world in which God lives. But the Bible has no place for such views. It never allows us to rank the spiritual above the physical. Matter matters because God made it; it is 'good'. He is interested not just in our souls but also in our bodies and the world we live in. As we shall see in the next chapter, human sin spoilt everything in the world, both the physical and the spiritual. In his grace God decided to put things right again, and he is determined not to do only half the job. His plan of salvation includes everything, spiritual and physical. Our look at the big picture of the Bible will take us on a journey from creation to new creation. God made everything in the beginning and he will redeem everything in the end. The Bible is heading towards a conclusion in heaven because that is the culmination of God's plan for his world. In many ways it will take us back to the beginning, to the way everything was designed to be in the first place: a new Eden.

2. God is the king of creation
As creator of all, God is Lord of all. He is the rightful king

over everything he has made. The only proper response to that truth is to acknowledge his rule and worship him. The psalmist writes:

> ... the LORD is the great God,
>   the great king above all gods.
> In his hands are the depths of the earth,
>   and the mountain peaks belong to him.
> The sea is his, for he made it,
>   and his hands formed the dry land.
>
> Come, let us bow down in worship,
>   let us kneel before the LORD our Maker;
> for he is our God
>   and we are the people of his pasture,
>   the flock under his care.
> (Psalm 95:3–7)

In much eastern religious thinking the natural world is believed to have emanated out of God. The result is that everything is a part of him. You dare not kill an ant or a fly: it is divine, along with trees, mountains, human beings and everything else you could mention. But the Bible will not allow such thinking. God is transcendent, above and beyond all that he has made and distinct from it. That truth explains the Bible's abhorrence of idolatry (see the second commandment, Exodus 20:4–6). If God made everything, then to worship anything within creation as if it were God is bound to demean him, because, by definition, it is less than him. God alone is worthy of worship. Our duty as his creatures is to submit to him as our king and give him the glory that rightly belongs to him.

> 'You are worthy, our Lord and God,
>   to receive glory and honour and power,
> for you created all things,

> and by your will they were created
> and have their being.'
> (Revelation 4:11)

3. Human beings are the pinnacle of creation

The anthropologist Desmond Morris has written: 'Human beings are animals. They are sometimes monsters, sometimes magnificent, but always animals.'[1] That statement is correct as far as it goes. We are creatures, made on the same day of creation as the beasts and sharing much in common with them. But we are not just animals, mere 'naked apes'. We alone, of all God's creation, have been made in his image:

> . . . God created man
> in his own image,
> in the image of God
> he created him;
> male and female
> he created them.
> (Genesis 1:27)

That is true of all people: male and female, black and white, young and old, born and unborn, able-bodied and disabled, whether mentally or physically.

Someone might say of a son, 'He's a chip off the old block; he's the spitting image of his father.' That is not to say he is identical, but he does bear the family likeness. You can see his father in him. It is similar with us and God. One writer has expressed it well: 'Man is a creature because he is made by God. But he is a unique creature, he is made like God.'[2] We reflect something of God's nature in a way that nothing else in creation does.

As those who have been made uniquely in God's image, all human beings have great dignity and have been set by him above the rest of the created order with responsibility for it. He said, '. . . let them rule over the fish of the sea and the birds of the air, over the livestock, over all the earth, and over all the creatures that move along the ground' (Genesis 1:26). That is certainly not a charter for abuse. God is a loving ruler and, as his image-bearers, we are called to rule in a loving way. We are God's stewards, entrusted with the care of his precious creation.

4. 'Rest' is the goal of creation

The chapter divisions of the Bible were inserted not by its authors but by editors at a later date. It is a shame that they ended Genesis 1 where they did, after the creation of men and women. That gives the impression that human beings are the climax of God's creation. But the real climax comes at the beginning of chapter 2, with the account of the seventh day:

> Thus the heavens and the earth were completed in all their vast array.
> By the seventh day God had finished the work he had been doing; so on the seventh day he rested from all his work. And God blessed the seventh day and made it holy, because on it he rested from all the work of creation that he had done.
> (Genesis 2:1–3)

The writer of Genesis ends his description of each of the other days with the words, 'And there was evening and there was morning – the first [etc.] day.' But no such end to the seventh day is recorded; it continues. In a sense, God has rested ever since. He lives in a continuing Sabbath, the seventh day. That does not mean that he is not working. He continues to sustain his creation; without him everything would fall apart. But he has rested from his work of creating. When a job has been done perfectly, there is nothing more to do. And he wants human beings to live with him in that seventh day, sharing in his 'rest' and enjoying his perfect creation. That is what we see happening in the verses that follow. Genesis 2:4–25 provide a second account of creation, not contradicting but complementing the first. In the first account human beings are just one of God's many creations, but in the second the focus is very much on them. It gives us a picture of the goal of creation; here is life as it was designed to be lived. It is marked by a series of perfect relationships.

God and human beings

God lovingly cares for the man he has made. He places him in a beautiful garden and provides for all his needs, including the creation of woman to be his helper and companion. Adam and Eve are given great responsibility, but there is no doubt about who is ultimately in charge. It is God who sets the rules. But his law is not oppressive; it is for their good. He issues just one prohibition, which is designed to protect them: ' . . . you must not eat from the tree of the knowledge of good and evil, for when you eat of it you will surely die' (Genesis 2:17).

Man and woman

Man is created first, then the woman as his helper. Man is the leader in the relationship,[3] but his authority is not abused and the woman does not resist it. They enjoy marital bliss: 'The man and his wife were both naked, and they felt no shame' (2:25). They have complete intimacy without fear or guilt.

Human beings and creation

Adam and Eve both exercise the authority God gave them over the created order but, once again, that authority is not abused. They obey God's instructions both to 'work' the land and to 'take care of it' (2:15). Human beings and creation work in harmony, so the earth brings forth its fruit.

The kingdom of God

It is an idyllic picture of the good life: life as it was meant to be. We see in the garden of Eden a pattern of the kingdom of God. God's people, Adam and Eve, live in God's place, the garden of Eden, under God's rule; as a result, they enjoy God's blessing.

Sadly, it is not long before everything is spoilt by human sin. Ever since, God has been at work to re-establish his kingdom and to call a people back into fellowship with himself. He wants us to enjoy the goal of creation and enter into the perfection of the seventh day, his rest. Part of the purpose of the Sabbath law (Exodus 20:8–11) was to remind the Israelites that that is ultimately what life was designed for, rather than the concerns of the present world. We can experience something of that rest even in this fallen world, if we trust in Jesus. He said, 'Come to me, all you who are weary and burdened and I will give you rest' (Matthew 11:28). And, as Christians, we can look forward to enjoying it fully in the new creation after Jesus returns. The writer to the Hebrews in the New Testament points us to the future with these encouraging words: 'There remains, then, a Sabbath-rest for the people of God; for anyone who enters God's rest also rests from his own work, just as God did from his' (Hebrews 4:9–10).

The kingdom of God	The pattern of the kingdom
God's people	Adam and Eve
God's place	The garden
God's rule and blessing	God's word; perfect relation-ships

Figure 7. The pattern of the kingdom

Bible study

Genesis 1:1 – 2:25

1:1–25
What are the repeated words and phrases?

What do they tell us about
- how God made the world?

- what God made?

- God the creator?

1:26–31
What does being in God's image mean?

Prince Charles once said about verse 28: 'It is a licence to exploit the environment. It has contributed to a feeling that the world is entirely man's to dispose of – as income, rather than as a capital asset which needs husbanding.' How would you respond to him?

2:1–25
What made the seventh day different from the previous six?

What are we told about the relationship of
- God and human beings?

- man and woman?

- human beings and creation?

In Hebrews 4:9–11 we are told that it is possible for us to enter God's rest. What does that mean?

Take a quick look at Revelation 22:1–5. What are the similarities with the garden of Eden?

The perished kingdom

A talking snake

Genesis 3 tells the sad story of how God's perfect creation is spoilt. It all begins with a talking snake: 'Now the serpent was more crafty than any of the wild animals the LORD God had made. He said to the woman, "Did God really say, 'You must not eat from any tree in the garden'?"' (Genesis 3:1).

That raises all sorts of questions straight away. Who is this serpent and where does he come from? And are we really expected to believe that this actually happened? Whoever heard of a snake that speaks?

The New Testament identifies the snake as Satan (Revelation 12:9; 20:2), but we are never told where he came from. He is certainly not eternal. The Bible gives no support for the kind of dualistic ideas that are found in some science-fiction films in which there is an eternal cosmic struggle between two equal forces of good and evil. Satan is certainly powerful, but he is not equal to God. God alone is eternal. It follows, therefore, that Satan is a created being. He was part of the original, perfect creation, but then he must have rebelled against God. On two occasions the New Testament speaks of a rebellion in the angelic world (2 Peter 2:4; Jude 6). But there is no mention of such things in Genesis 3. The writer does not set out to answer all our questions; he simply tells us what we need to know. It does not matter whether or not we understand where evil comes from, but it is important that we know of its existence.

How we are meant to understand Genesis 3? Is the account of the fall a myth with no basis in fact, or did it actually happen? The rest of the Bible assumes that it was a real event. Paul compares and contrasts Adam and the Lord Jesus (Romans 5:12–19; 1 Corinthians 15:20–22). Just as Jesus was a real human being, whose death achieved a real salvation, so Adam was a real human being, whose sin resulted in a real fall: '... since death came through a man, the resurrection of the dead comes also through a man' (1 Corinthians 15:21). That still leaves the question of the talking snake. Are we meant to take that literally? That depends on the kind of literature we think the author was writing. My own view, for what it's worth, is that Genesis 3 describes an actual event but uses some symbolism as it does so.[1]

An act of rebellion

God exercised his rule in the garden through his word and that is where Satan directs his attack. He begins by distorting it and making it sound harsher than it is: 'Did God really say, "You must not eat from any tree in the garden"?' (verse 1).

Eve soon puts him right; they had been forbidden to eat from only one tree: 'God did say, "You must not eat fruit from the tree that is in the middle of the garden, and you must not touch it, or you will die"' (verse 3).

Satan still does not give up. He now starts to question God's word: 'You will not surely die' (verse 4). He even makes God out to be a cosmic spoilsport: 'God knows that when you eat of it your eyes will be opened, and you will be like God, knowing good and evil' (verse 5).

The tactics work: 'When the woman saw that the fruit of

the tree was good for food and pleasing to the eye, and also desirable for gaining wisdom, she took some and ate it. She also gave some to her husband, who was with her, and he ate it' (verse 6).

Why was that so terrible? What is wrong with eating a bit of fruit? It is wrong because God told them not to; it was an act of blatant disobedience. But why did God not want them to eat from the tree of the knowledge of good and evil? Surely it is good to know the difference between right and wrong? Yes, but the 'knowledge of good and evil' refers not simply to knowing what is right and wrong, but rather to *deciding* what is right and wrong. Their sin is that of law-making, not just law-breaking. They were saying, 'From now on, God, we want to be the law-makers in the world, setting the standards by which we will live.' It was a bid to be like God, but not in any noble sense. They were usurping his authority and establishing their independence. That has been the nature of sin ever since.

Broken relationships
The consequences are disastrous. God acts in judgment to spoil all the perfect relationships that were established at creation.

The relationship between men and women
The perfect trust and intimacy have now gone. They make coverings to hide their nakedness (verse 7). And it is not long before they start squabbling, as neither will accept responsibility for their actions. The battle of the sexes has begun. God tells the woman, 'Your desire will be for your husband, and he will rule over you' (verse 16). God tells the woman, 'your desire will be for your husband and he will rule over you' (verse 16). The woman 'desires' her husband. The word may simply refer to sexual desire, but it may also suggest a longing to take control over him (the word is used in that sense in Genesis 4:7). If so, we are being told that the woman will no longer submit willingly to her husband's lead and he will no longer exercise it in the loving, self-sacrificial

way that was God's design. The loving primacy of Genesis 2 is now replaced by harsh 'rule'.

The relationship between human beings and creation

The harmony between human beings and the created order is ended. From now on it will be a struggle to control it. God says,

> 'Cursed is the ground because of you;
>> through painful toil you will eat of it
>> all the days of your life.
> It will produce thorns and thistles for you,
>> and you will eat the plants of the field.'
> (3:17–18)

Working the land will now involve much sweat and hard labour. The natural world is to be experienced not just as a friend but also as an enemy.

The relationship between human beings and God

The punishment fits the crime. Human beings turn away from God in rebellion and he turns away from them in judgment. The warm friendship they had enjoyed with God is now destroyed. When he draws near, they hide from him. God still comes looking for them: ' . . . the Lord God called to the man, "Where are you?"' (verse 9). In his grace God continues to seek after sinful human beings, calling us back into fellowship with him; but by nature we always run away. Adam is afraid and ashamed, conscious of his nakedness before God. The old innocence has gone. And God judges the guilty, just as he had said he would. Satan was wrong. God's warning that Adam and Eve would die was no mere threat; it is carried out. They are banished from the garden and a guard is placed to prevent them from returning to the tree of life (verse 24). They continue to exist physically, but spiritually they are dead, cut off from God's presence. It is only a matter of time before their physical existence also ends.

The spread of sin and death

Ever since the fall, all human beings have been born facing the same predicament as Adam and Eve: spiritual and physical death because of the rebellion of our ancestors. We too are sinners, rebels against God's rule; and we too face the punishment of death, eternal separation from him. Chapters 4 – 11 of Genesis chart the spread of sin and of death, God's judgment against it, in the first period of human history.

Cain and Abel (chapter 4)

It is no surprise that the account of the sin of Adam and Eve in chapter 3 is followed by the account of the first murder in the very next chapter as one of their sons murders his brother. Once the vertical relationship with God has been broken, it is inevitable that horizontal relationships with one another will be broken as well. Cain is jealous that his brother found favour with God, and he kills him. God's judgment swiftly follows. Cain is sent away from home and condemned to a life of wandering.

Mortality (chapter 5)

Genesis 5 contains the first genealogy in the Bible. Human beings are obeying God's command to 'be fruitful and increase in number' (1:28). Even after the fall, their offspring still bear the image of God. The writer stresses that just as Adam was created in the 'likeness of God', so his son Seth was in his 'likeness' (verses 1–3). But it is a marred image. Human beings also bear the marks of sin. As a result, just as in chapter 4 sin was passed down to the next generation, so we find in chapter 5 that its consequence, death, is also inherited. Those early humans may have lived for many years, but a refrain that runs through the chapter reminds us that they were mortal: 'and then he died ... and then he died ... and then he died ...' (verses 5, 8, 11, etc.). We do all we can to blunt the harsh reality of death. We even try to avoid mentioning the word. I heard recently of a hospital in America that refers to death as 'negative patient care outcome'.

But, for all our euphemisms, we cannot avoid death. It comes to us all.

The flood (chapters 6 – 9)

A few generations have come and gone, but sin is very much alive. The writer makes a devastating comment: 'The LORD saw how great man's wickedness on the earth had become, and that every inclination of the thoughts of his heart was only evil all the time. The LORD was grieved that he had made man on the earth, and his heart was filled with pain' (verses 5–6). He therefore resolves to act in judgment: 'The LORD said, "I will wipe mankind, whom I have created, from the face of the earth – men and animals, and creatures that move along the ground, and birds of the air – for I am grieved that I have made them"' (verse 7). The resulting flood causes terrible destruction. It is a reversal of creation. The division between earth and the waters, which God established on the first day of creation, is undone. There is a return to the chaos which existed before the world was made, as, once again, water covers the earth (see Genesis 1:2).

The Tower of Babel (chapter 11)

God preserved one family through the flood, so human history continued. But, sadly, so did sin and God's righteous response to it, namely judgment. Chapter 11 brings us to the lowest point in the Bible so far. Human beings proudly say, 'Come, let us build ourselves a city, with a tower that reaches to the heavens, so that we may make a name for ourselves and not be scattered over the face of the whole earth' (verse 4). The tower of Babel is a vivid symbol of our sinful desire to exalt ourselves and create our own kingdom independently of God. But he will not ignore such arrogance. He frustrates the people's empire-building by scattering them throughout the earth and giving them different languages. Human beings are now divided not just from God but from one another.

The perished kingdom

The perfect creation that God had established is now nothing but a distant dream. The pattern of the kingdom has been destroyed by sin. Human beings are no longer God's people by nature; we have turned away from him. We no longer live in his place; we have been banished from the garden. And we reject his rule and live as if we ruled the world. God continues to reign, but he reigns in judgment. As a result, we do not enjoy God's blessing but instead face his curse. It is all so sad. A perfect world has been destroyed by human rebellion (Figure 8).

The kingdom of God	The pattern of the kingdom	The perished kingdom
God's people	Adam and Eve	No-one
God's place	The garden	Banished
God's rule and blessing	God's word; perfect relationships	Disobedience and curse

Figure 8. The perished kingdom

The story goes on

That is where the Bible could have ended. There is no reason why God should do anything to help us. But he is a gracious God, who is determined to put things right again and to restore his kingdom on earth. He continues to rule, of course; nothing changes that. He is the sovereign God, who is in control even when people disobey him. But he wants to bring back to himself a people who willingly submit to his rule. That is what is meant by 'the kingdom of God': not the area where he rules (for he always rules everywhere) but the sphere where his rule is gladly accepted. As we shall see in the next chapter, God works towards that wonderful end right from the very beginning.

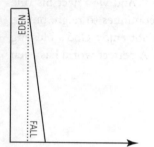

Figure 9. The story so far: the fall

 Bible study

Genesis 3

The serpent (verses 1–5)
What tactics does the serpent use to tempt Eve?

How do we see him using the same tactics today?

The sin (verse 6)

What did Adam and Eve do wrong?

In what way are we guilty of the same sin?

The shame (verses 7–13)

What immediate impact does Adam and Eve's sin have on
- their relationship with God?

- their relationship with others (compare 2:22–25)?

The sentence (verses 14–24)

What does God's punishment mean for
- the serpent?

- the woman?

- the man?

- all human beings?

The Saviour
What signs of hope can we see in the passage?

3

The promised kingdom

God's eternal plan

> Praise be to the God and Father of our Lord Jesus Christ,
> who has blessed us in the heavenly realms with every
> spiritual blessing in Christ. For he chose us in him before the
> creation of the world to be holy and blameless in his sight.
> In love he predestined us to be adopted as his sons through
> Jesus Christ, in accordance with his pleasure and will – to the
> praise of his glorious grace, which he has freely given us in
> the One he loves.
> (Ephesians 1:3–6)

Ephesians 1 is mind-blowing in its scope. It takes us from eternity
to eternity; from before the creation of the world to after its end.
The apostle Paul gives us an insight into the eternal plan of God.
He is certainly not defeated by the fall. Before the disobedience of
Adam and Eve, before they or anything else even existed, God
had already decided on a rescue operation. He had determined
from eternity to call a people to himself through his Son Jesus and

to restore everything under him: 'to bring all things in heaven and on earth together under one head, even Christ' (verse 10).

Of course, there is mystery here. If God knew it would happen, why did he allow the fall to happen in the first place? The Bible gives no answer to that question. It just tells us what we need to know: God is in control. It gives us a certain hope that one day the awful consequences of our rebellion against him will be undone. As a result, he will be honoured and glorified. Paul stresses that this is why he decided to rescue the world: for 'the praise of his glorious grace' (verse 6); 'for the praise of his glory' (verses 12, 14). His motivation was not, first and foremost, to make us happy, although that is certainly one final result. Above all, he was concerned for his name. It sounds dreadfully egotistical to us, but there is nothing selfish about it. In wanting his world to praise him, God is not looking for an ego boost; he is rather seeking to restore things to the way they should be.

Two boys were bored on a rainy summer's day, so they began to do a jigsaw puzzle. That tells you how bored they must have been. They made no progress until one of them turned the box lid over to see the picture they were trying to create. It was of a medieval court scene with a king surrounded by his courtiers. One of the boys cried out, 'Now I see it – the king is in the middle!' Once they recognized that, the puzzle was easy and they were soon able to finish it.

Just as the king was in the middle of that picture, so God is in the centre of the world that he has made. But, since the fall, human beings have refused to accept his right to be there and have tried to depose him. The results have been catastrophic: everything is spoiled. But we need not despair. From before the creation, God has had a plan to put the world right by re-establishing his kingdom through his Son, the Lord Jesus, so that once more he is glorified. And, when the King is in the middle, everything else falls into place.

As God's plan of salvation is eternal, it is no surprise to see hints of it even during the dark days of the fall and its immediate aftermath; even then the bright light of the gospel can be seen. It gives hope in the midst of despair and begins to promise better things to come.

Amazing grace

In the last chapter we noticed the theme of sin and judgment (death) running through the early chapters of Genesis. But there is a third theme too: grace. Human sin is met by God's judgment, but he also shows great mercy (Figure 10).

Sin ⟹ Judgment ⟹ GRACE

Figure 10. Grace

The serpent-crusher (3:15)

Adam and Eve's disobedience results in their banishment from the garden. But Genesis 3 is not all doom and gloom. Despite their sin, God still loves them. He comes looking for them and then provides clothes for them to hide their nakedness (verse 21). His love is seen above all in a promise he makes while judging the serpent:

> 'I will put enmity
> > between you and the woman,
> > and between your offspring and hers;
> he will crush your head,
> > and you will strike his heel.'
> (3:15)

It is only a hint, but it is a very encouraging one. God seems to be pointing to a time in the future when a son of Eve, a human being, will destroy the evil one. It is a veiled prophecy of the work of the Lord Jesus. He inflicted defeat on Satan through his death on the cross and will return to complete the job. Paul echoes the words of Genesis 3:15 when he tells us: 'The God of peace will soon crush Satan under your feet' (Romans 16:20).

The mark of Cain (4:15)

After killing Abel, Cain is driven into exile. But God does not completely abandon him. He places a protective mark on Cain and promises that anyone who kills him will himself be judged.

'Enoch walked with God' (5:24)

The genealogy of chapter 5 underlines how the punishment of death faces each generation. But the depressing refrain, 'and then he died ... and then he died ...', is missing in verse 24. The account of every other life ends with those words, but Enoch's is different: 'Enoch walked with God; then he was no more, because God took him away.' We are given hope that, even in a fallen world, it is possible to know God and escape the penalty of death.

God's covenant with Noah (6:18; 9:1–17)

Genesis 6:8 is best translated, 'Noah found grace in the eyes of the LORD.' We have just been told that all people are sinful (verse 5), and that certainly included Noah. But God chose him and his family to be recipients of grace. He said, 'I will make a covenant with you, and you will enter the ark – you and your sons and your wife and your sons' wives with you' (6:18). 'Covenant' is a very important word in the Bible (see Figure 11). It speaks of a binding agreement. God promises Noah that he will rescue his family from the flood in the ark. Noah believes God, acts on his word and is saved when the waters rise. Then, when they have receded, God makes another promise: 'I establish my covenant with you: Never again will all life be cut off by the waters of a flood; never again will there be a flood to destroy the earth' (9:11). Although human sin continues, God declares his commitment to creation. God has not finished with his world; he is determined to fulfil his eternal plan. The flood was an undoing of the created order, but it was followed by a gracious restoration; a new start. That fact is underlined by the repetition of phrases from the creation account in God's words after the flood (Figure 12).

Covenant is one of the most important concepts in the Bible. It is found in our names for the two parts of Scripture: Old and New Testament ('testament' is another word for covenant) and the word appears frequently (285 times in the OT and 33 in the NT). It refers to a solemn commitment. God commits himself to his people by making binding promises. Sometimes they are unilateral (God promises to act unconditionally), but often they are bilateral and conditional: God expects his people to make their own promises to obey him. The covenants are sealed in blood and are given with a sign that is designed to be a reminder of them. The Bible contains a number of covenants:

The Noahic covenant

God makes a unilateral covenant to preserve his creation and never again to destroy it by a flood.

Sign: a rainbow

The Abrahamic covenant

God promises to raise up a great nation from Abraham's descendants and give them a land to live in. He will bless them and through them the whole world will be blessed.

Sign: circumcision

The Mosaic covenant

God promises the Israelites that they will be his special people; they, in turn, are commanded to obey his law.

Sign: the Sabbath

The new covenant

The Israelites break their covenant obligations and God has to judge them. But he promises through the prophet Jeremiah a new and better covenant, which leads to a changed heart, universal knowledge of God and complete forgiveness. Jesus' death on the cross inaugurates this new covenant.

Sign: baptism

These covenants are distinct but they are also bound together. They are all part of God's eternal plan to save the world through Jesus.

Figure 11. Covenant

Genesis 1	Genesis 9
'Be fruitful and increase in number; fill the earth' (verse 28)	'Be fruitful and increase in number and fill the earth' (verse 1)
'Subdue [the earth]. Rule over . . . every living creature that moves on the ground' (verse 28)	'The fear and dread of you will fall upon all the beasts of the earth . . . ' (verse 2)
'I give you every seed-bearing plant on the face of the whole earth . . . for food' (verse 29)	'Everything that lives and moves will be food for you' (verse 3)

Figure 12. The flood: a new start

Having made his promise, God puts a sign in the sky: a rainbow. Whenever he sees it in the future, he will remember his commitment to creation (9:14–15) And whenever we see it, we are to take comfort.

The covenant with Abraham

In every episode in the early chapters of Genesis, after the fall, we have noticed the three elements of sin, judgment and grace. But the account of the tower of Babel seems to be an exception. Sin and judgment are both there as the people build the tower and are then scattered and divided from one another. But there is no sign of God's grace in Genesis 11. We have to wait until the next chapter and another generation. God appears to Abraham and promises to reverse the effects of his judgment after Babel. He declares his intention to bring back the scattered people of the world and to bless them once more. His words to Abraham are the first clear statement of God's promises, the gospel; they will dominate the rest of the Bible. John Stott has written: 'It may truly be said without exaggeration that not only the rest of the Old Testament but the whole of the New Testament are an outworking of these promises of God.'[1] Genesis 12:1–3 is the text the rest of the Bible expounds:

> The LORD had said to Abram, 'Leave your country, your people, and your father's household and go to the land I will show you.
>
> 'I will make you into a great nation
>   and I will bless you;
> I will make your name great,
>   and you will be a blessing.
> I will bless those who bless you,
>   and whoever curses you I will curse;
> and all peoples on earth
>   will be blessed through you.'

There was nothing particularly special about Abraham. He was chosen not because of his goodness but because of God's grace alone. There are three main elements to the promises he received: people, land, and blessing.

People
Abraham's descendants will become a great nation that will be God's own people. This is later underlined when God says, 'I will establish my covenant as an everlasting covenant between me and you and your descendants after you for the generations to come, to be your God and the God of your descendants after you' (Genesis 17:7). The promise is frequently repeated throughout the Old Testament in the covenant refrain, 'I will be your God and you will be my people.'

Land
Abraham is commanded to leave his homeland and to go to another land that God will show him. This is Canaan, the promised land. God says to Abraham, 'The whole land of Canaan, where you

are now an alien, I will give as an everlasting possession to you and your descendants after you' (17:8).

Blessing

Abraham's descendants will be blessed, and through them 'all peoples on earth will be blessed'. The curse of the fall would be replaced by the blessing of salvation. Right from the very start God's plan of salvation was universal; it encompassed all nations. This fact was underlined when God changed the patriarch's name from Abram (which means 'exalted father') to Abraham ('father of a multitude') (17:5).

This great covenant came with a sign. Every male Israelite child was to be circumcised (17:10–11). They thus bore in their own bodies a mark that signified the special relationship established between God and his people.

The promised kingdom

The covenant with Abraham is a promise of the kingdom of God: God's people (Abraham's descendants) in God's place (the promised land) under God's rule and therefore enjoying his blessing. It is a promise to reverse the effects of the fall.

It must have been hard for Abraham to believe that it would all take place, but he did: 'Abram believed the LORD, and he credited it to him as righteousness' (15:6). He was accepted by God, not on the basis of his own goodness, but by faith in the promises of God. That has always been the way of salvation for sinful human beings. We can never deserve a place in God's family. Our only hope is to trust in the gospel. It is the same for us as it was for Abraham. As we shall see in the next chapter, the gospel that was first proclaimed to him was partially fulfilled, in the history of Israel, in the promised land of Canaan. But that same gospel has now been finally fulfilled in Jesus Christ. He, and those from all nations who trust in him, are God's people; and we can look forward to enjoying the fullness of God's blessing, not on earth, but in heaven, the new Jerusalem (Figure 13).

The kingdom of God	The pattern of the kingdom	The perished kingdom	The promised kingdom
God's people	Adam and Eve	No-one	Abraham's descendants
God's place	The garden	Banished	Canaan
God's rule and blessing	God's word; perfect relationships	Disobedience and curse	Blessing to Israel and the nations

Figure 13. The promised kingdom

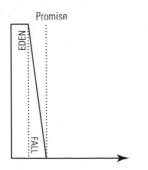

Figure 14. The story so far: promise

Bible study

Genesis 17:1–8; Galatians 3:6–14

Genesis 17:1–8
God confirms the covenant by repeating his promises. List them under these three headings:

People

Land

Blessing

Galatians 3:6–14
The Galatian Christians are being led astray by false teaching that suggests that it is not enough to believe in Christ but that they also need to obey the Jewish law if they are to be right with God. Paul counters this teaching by pointing them to Abraham.

Why are those who have faith in Christ Abraham's true children?

What does it mean to 'rely on observing the law' (verse 10)? How might we do that today?

Why is it futile?

How is it possible for us to receive God's blessing instead of the curse of judgment?

How would you explain the truths of this passage to a non-Christian?

4

The partial kingdom

You may be wondering if we shall ever reach the end of our journey through the Bible. The first three chapters have taken us only a quarter of the way through Genesis. That still leaves a long way to travel: there are sixty-five and three-quarter books left. It was important, however, that we looked at the beginning of the Bible in some detail. It lays the foundations that are essential if we are to understand the rest of it. But don't worry; we shall be moving at a much faster pace from now on. Many books of the Bible will hardly get a mention, if at all. The aim is not to get lost in detail but rather to see the sweep of the Bible's storyline: the big picture.

I should start with a warning: this will be a long chapter. That is hardly surprising. We shall be covering the history of Israel from Abraham until the high point of the monarchy under Solomon: a period of over 1,000 years. There are four main elements to the promise of the kingdom of God. We have seen three of them already: people, land and blessing. A fourth is added later: the promise of a king. The aim of this chapter is to see how God's promise of the kingdom is partially fulfilled in the history of

Israel. The chapter will be divided into four main sections as we look at the fulfilment of each promise in turn. At some points of this section of the Bible the fulfilment of more than one promise is in view, but, broadly speaking, it is fair to say that the focus of Genesis 12 to Exodus 18 is the 'people' promise; Exodus 19 to the end of Leviticus, the 'rule and blessing' promise; Numbers to Joshua, the 'land' promise; and Judges to 2 Chronicles, the 'king' promise (Figure 15).

God's people	Genesis 12 to Exodus 18
God's rule and blessing	Exodus 19 to Leviticus
God's place/land	Numbers to Joshua
God's king	Judges to 2 Chronicles

Figure 15. The promise and the history of Israel

God's people: Genesis 12 – Exodus 18

The promise

'I will make you into a great nation.'
(Genesis 12:2)

'I will take you as my own people, and I will be your God.'
(Exodus 6:7)

The partial fulfilment

Abraham and Isaac

The focus of Genesis 12 to Exodus 18 is on how God fulfils his promise to Abraham, that his descendants will be a great nation, and brings the nation of Israel into being as his very own people

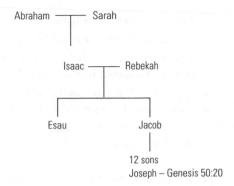

Figure 16. The patriarchs

(see Figure 16). But that does not happen smoothly; there are problems at every turn. The first problem is a fundamental one: Abraham's wife Sarah is barren and they have no children. The gospel promises are in danger of failing almost as soon as they have been made. Abraham decides it is time to take matters into his own hands, and sleeps with Sarah's maid, Hagar, who gives birth to a son, Ishmael. But God makes it clear that his people will not arise from Ishmael. Abraham has to learn that, if the gospel is to be fulfilled, only God can bring it about. Abraham must simply trust in God's promise. We today need to understand exactly the same truth: 'it is by grace you have been saved, through faith – and this not from yourselves, it is the gift of God – not by works, so that no-one can boast' (Ephesians 2:8–9).

The years continue to pass and Sarah still does not conceive, but one day God speaks to Abraham and reassures him that, despite her great age, she will bear a son. And, sure enough, it happens. I once heard a friend of mine invite us to imagine the scene at the local hospital. Sarah, aged ninety, hobbles to the entrance with her Zimmer frame. A kind nurse greets her: 'Hello dear, is it the Geriatric Department you are after?'

'No,' Sarah replies, 'I want the Maternity Ward.'

'How lovely!' says the nurse. 'Have you come to see a great-grandchild?'

'No,' says Sarah, 'I've come to have a baby.'

You can imagine the nurses having a good laugh at that over their coffee break. They were not the first to laugh at the idea. Abraham also laughed when God told him it would happen. That is why the boy was given the name Isaac, which means 'he laughs'. It was a laughable idea; it is impossible for a ninety-year-old woman to give birth. But it happened. Right at this early stage we are being taught that it will take a miracle for the gospel to be fulfilled.

At last the gospel train is beginning to move forward. There is still a long way to go before it reaches its destination in Jesus, but at least the journey has begun. But almost as soon as it is out of the station it looks as if it will be derailed. God tells Abraham to sacrifice Isaac (Genesis 22). It is an extraordinary command. What hope is there if Isaac dies? Abraham did not understand why God told him to do it, and he was full of grief at the thought, but he was still prepared to obey. We should not understand this incident simply as a demonstration of the wholehearted obedience of Abraham. Above all, it reveals his faith in God's promises. He knew that the future of the promises depended on Isaac's survival, so he trusted that God would protect his son somehow, or even raise him from the dead (see Hebrews 11:17–19). His faith was well placed. At the last minute, God provided a ram to be killed instead of Isaac. We need to learn from Abraham's example and trust in the gospel promises even when we cannot understand what God is doing in our lives.

Jacob and Esau

Abraham dies and the future of the promise now focuses on Isaac. He marries Rebekah and they have two sons, Jacob and Esau. Esau is the oldest son and yet it is Jacob who receives his father's blessing. He is the one whose descendants will be in the line of promise and become the people of God. Why does God choose him? He is certainly not the obvious choice: he is the younger son and a most unpleasant character too. His name sums him up:

'deceiver'. It is through trickery that he is blessed by the old man Isaac (Genesis 27). Once again we learn a principle that operates right through the Bible: God does not choose people on merit. None of us will ever deserve to belong to him. Paul writes in Romans: 'Rebekah's children had one and the same father, our father Isaac. Yet, before the twins were born or had done anything good or bad – in order that God's purpose in election might stand: not by works but by him who calls – she was told, "The older will serve the younger"' (9:10–13). If we are Christians today, it is not because we are better than anyone else; it is simply because of God's sovereign choice.

Joseph

Jacob has twelve sons. They are far from being a great nation, but the promise is beginning to be fulfilled. They are not a very attractive bunch. Joseph is his father's favourite and his brothers are jealous of him. They sell him as a slave and tell Jacob he is dead. Joseph ends up in Egypt and is soon sent to jail for something he has not done.

He must often wonder in his imprisonment, 'Is God really in control?' There is very little evidence of it. But God knows what he is doing. If Joseph had not been in jail he would not have met Pharaoh's cupbearer, who, on his release, is able to tell Pharaoh about Joseph's ability to interpret dreams. He is summoned to the royal court and correctly interprets Pharaoh's dreams, warning him of a coming famine. Joseph is released, made Prime Minister of Egypt and takes measures that protect the country from the effects of the famine.

Canaan, where Jacob and his sons live, is not so fortunate. The famine threatens to kill them, which would mean the end of any hope of the gospel being fulfilled. They go to Egypt to try to buy some food and come face to face with the brother they have so mistreated. Not surprisingly, they are terrified when he reveals his true identity. What will he do to them? But he reassures them: 'Don't be afraid. Am I in the place of God? You intended to harm me, but God intended it for good to accomplish what is now being done, the saving of many lives' (Genesis 50:19–20).

God has been in control all along. He has seen to it that Joseph is in Egypt and has risen to high office so that he can be in a position to help when his brothers come, and, as a result, the embryonic people of God is preserved.

God always overrules to ensure that his gospel promises are protected. We may not always understand how he does that. We may feel there were easier ways in which God could have protected his people in Joseph's day. Why not just keep the famine from affecting Canaan, rather than allowing Joseph to be enslaved and imprisoned? But even when we do not understand God's purposes, we can be sure that they are loving ones and that they always guarantee that his will is done. Nothing, whether human evil, terrible famine, or anything else, can prevent God from fulfilling his gospel promises.

'I am who I am'

Jacob and his family all move to Egypt to be with Joseph and settle there. By the beginning of the book of Exodus their hosts have enslaved their descendants and they are cruelly treated. God must set them free if they are to be his people as he promised. Through the long years of slavery they must wonder if he has forgotten the promise, but God can never do that. 'The Israelites groaned in their slavery and cried out, and their cry for help because of their slavery went up to God. God heard their groaning and he remembered his covenant with Abraham, with Isaac and with Jacob. So God looked on the Israelites and was concerned about them' (Exodus 2:23–25).

God begins his rescue operation by appearing to Moses in a burning bush at Horeb (another name for Sinai). He tells him to go to Pharaoh to demand the release of his people. And he reveals a new name to Moses: 'I AM WHO I AM' or 'I WILL BE WHAT I WILL BE' (Exodus 3:14).

There are no vowels in the Hebrew (YHWH), which makes it

impossible to know exactly what the word is. Some old translations say 'Jehovah'. Modern scholars tend to speak of 'Yahweh'. When the word appears in our English versions of the Bible it almost always does so as 'LORD' in capital letters. It is a strange name for God to give himself. He seems to be saying that no one name can encapsulate his character. If we want to know who he is, we must watch him act in history on behalf of his people. 'I WILL BE WHAT I WILL BE. Do you want to know who I am, Moses? Then watch me; see what I will do in the future. Then you will know what kind of God I am.'

The Bible does not just tell the story of God's work of salvation; at the same time it reveals God's character. He is its hero from beginning to end. Sometimes we miss the point by asking too quickly, 'What is it saying to me?' A good first question to ask whenever we look at a passage is, 'What does this tell me about God?' Very often the application for us will then be obvious. The Bible is, above all, a book about God.

Salvation by substitution (the Passover)
Moses appears before Pharaoh and delivers God's command that his people should be set free. Pharaoh replies with contempt: 'Who is the LORD [Yahweh], that I should obey him and let Israel go?' (Exodus 5:2). He will soon find out. God sends ten terrible plagues against Egypt. They demonstrate the Lord's mighty power. Each time, Pharaoh stubbornly refuses to let the Israelites go, but the tenth and final plague breaks his resistance. On one dreadful night, God passes through the land in judgment and every Egyptian firstborn son is killed. The Israelite firstborn deserve to die as well; they too are sinners. But God graciously provides them with a way of escape. Each family is to kill a lamb instead and put its blood on the door-frame of their house. Moses tells them, 'When the LORD goes through the land to strike down the Egyptians, he will see the blood on the top and sides of the door-frame and will pass over that doorway, and he will not permit the destroyer to enter your houses and strike you down' (Exodus 12:23).

In this, the great act of God's salvation in the Old Testament era, the Israelites are being taught an important principle: God saves by substitution. His people deserve to die for their sin, but another dies instead. We are being prepared for a greater act of deliverance, of which the Passover is only a shadow. Just as the Passover lamb died for the sins of others, so Jesus died as a substitute. When John the Baptist saw him he said, 'Look, the Lamb of God, who takes away the sin of the world!' (John 1:29). It is no coincidence that Jesus died at Passover time (Matthew 26:19; John 19:31). The deliverance of the Israelites from Egypt points forward to the greater deliverance Jesus achieved on the cross. Paul explicitly says, 'Christ, our Passover lamb, has been sacrificed' (1 Corinthians 5:7).

Salvation by conquest (the crossing of the Sea)

Pharaoh has second thoughts as soon as he lets his slaves go. He sends his army to pursue them and they soon catch up. The situation is not good. The Israelites face the 'Red Sea' (probably a stretch of water at the northern end of the Suez Gulf) and the Egyptian soldiers are behind them. They are powerless to save themselves, but God intervenes. He parts the sea so that the Israelites can walk through it. But, when the Egyptians follow, the sea returns and drowns them.

Pharaoh certainly knows who the Lord is now. He has saved his people by defeating their oppressor and has revealed himself to be the sovereign God, more powerful than the forces of humankind and nature.

Once again, that act of salvation foreshadowed what God achieved through the death of Jesus. We were enslaved to the powers of sin and the devil, but God defeated them through the cross and has set us free. Paul writes: ' . . . having disarmed the powers and authorities [evil spiritual forces], he made a public spectacle of them, triumphing over them by the cross' (Colossians 2:15).

God's people

The Israelites do not travel straight to the promised land. Instead, they go to meet with God at Mount Sinai, where God had appeared to Moses in the bush. God says to them, 'You yourselves have seen what I did to Egypt, and how I carried you on eagles' wings and brought you to myself' (Exodus 19:4). By his act of salvation he has set them free from the Egyptians and made them his own special people. The 'people promise' has been fulfilled. But there is more to come. The exodus from Egypt is not the climax of the book that is named after it; it occupies only the first eighteen chapters. The rest of the book focuses on the giving of the law and the establishment of the tabernacle. God is not just a God who delivers; he is also a God who demands and who draws near. He wants to bless his people.

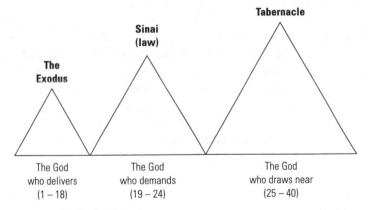

Figure 17. The book of Exodus

God's rule and blessing

The promise

> 'I will bless you.'
> (Genesis 12:2)

The partial fulfilment

We tend to have a negative attitude to authority and assume that it must always be oppressive. Bur there is nothing negative about being under God's authority. In the Bible, to be under God's rule is to enjoy God's blessing. When Adam and Eve obeyed God's command not to eat from the tree of the knowledge of good and evil, they knew life at its best: they enjoyed a relationship with their creator in his presence in the garden of Eden. God's law was for their good. It was only once they disobeyed it that they faced God's curse and were banished from his presence: he cannot continue to live among those who have rebelled against him. So, if the Israelites are to know God's blessing, they must be brought back under God's rule. Only then will they be able to enjoy a relationship with him and know his presence with them. If the rejection of God's law brings death and curse (separation from God), the restoration of the law enables life and blessing (relationship with God as he draws near again). The 'blessing promise' is therefore chiefly fulfilled in this period of the history of Israel in two ways: by the giving of God's law on Mount Sinai and then by his presence with his people in the tabernacle.

God's law

The law is given by God on Mount Sinai. It is not intended to be the means by which anyone gets right with God. The Israelites are already God's people through his grace. God reminds them of that truth in his introduction to the Ten Commandments. Before he states any of his laws, he begins by saying, 'I am the LORD your God, who brought you out of Egypt, out of the land of slavery' (Exodus 20:2). He redeems them before they receive the law. Their obedience is not to be a desperate attempt to earn his salvation; it is a response to the salvation he has already achieved for them. But if obedience to the law is not the path to membership in the covenant people of God, it is required for the enjoyment of blessing within the covenant. God promises to bless his people; they in turn must obey him: ' . . . if you obey me

The law reveals our sin. ' . . . no-one will be declared righteous in [God's] sight by observing the law; rather, through the law we become conscious of sin' (Romans 3:20).

The law reveals our Saviour. ' . . . we were held prisoners by the law, locked up until faith should be revealed. So the law was put in charge to lead us to Christ' (Galatians 3:23–24). The law's role was to prepare us for Christ. It convicts us of our sin and helps us to see our need of Jesus, the Saviour. Although he always obeyed the law, he faced the punishment for law-breaking in the place of others: 'Christ redeemed us from the curse of the law by becoming a curse for us' (Galatians 3:13).

The law reveals God's standards. The law not only points us to our sin and our Saviour; it also tells us how God wants us to live. Jesus commands his followers to obey its demands (Matthew 5:17–20). Whenever possible, we should work for the application of God's standards in the public realm too: in the workplace, at college and in society at large.[1]

Figure 18. God's law in the Bible

fully and keep my covenant, then out of all nations you will be my treasured possession' (Exodus 19:5).

As God's people they must live in a certain way. When the future George VI was a young boy, his mother, Queen Mary, often used to remind him before a public event, 'Bertie, never forget who you are.' He was a royal prince and should behave accordingly. In a similar way, God's 'holy nation,' set apart to belong to him, should reflect the character of the holy God. He tells them, ' . . . be holy, because I am holy' (Leviticus 11:44). The law is designed to teach them what that means in practice. Jesus said that all its commands rest on two principles: 'Love the Lord your God with all your heart and with all your soul and with all your mind' and 'Love your neighbour as yourself' (Matthew 22:37, 39).

God's presence

Now that God's people are under his rule again, they are able once more to enjoy his presence. The purpose of redemption is relationship. God instructs Moses how to construct the tabernacle, the tent in which his presence is to be focused among them as they travel towards the promised land (Figure 19).

The tabernacle consists of a courtyard and a tent inside, separated into two sections: 'The Holy Place' and 'the Most Holy Place' or 'Holy of Holies'. Inside the Holy Place is a table that holds 'the bread of the presence', twelve loaves of bread. It reminds them that God will provide for all their needs. Alongside it is a golden lampstand, which symbolizes God's constant watch over them to keep them from harm, and an altar of incense, which is intended to give a sense of the nearness of God. A curtain, or 'veil', screens the entrance to the Most Holy Place. There is just one piece of furniture inside: the ark. If the table speaks of the provision of God and the lampstand of his protection, the ark speaks of his presence. It is a chest, about 130 cm long and 60 cm wide and high. Inside are the stone tablets on which God has inscribed the Ten Commandments. Above it is a separate lid, which has been called 'the mercy seat' or 'atonement cover'. At either end are representations of a cherub (a heavenly creature). The wings of the cherubim above the ark spread horizontally over the cover to form the throne of the invisible God. God tells Moses, 'There, above the cover between the two cherubim that are over the ark of the Testimony, I will meet with you' (Exodus 25:22). His 'glory' fills the place and stays with them (Exodus 40:34–38). God is among his people once again.

Sacrifices

God's presence with his people is wonderful, but it also creates a problem. How can the holy God live among a sinful people without destroying them? From the very start the Israelites could not keep God's law, and deserved to face his judgment as a result.

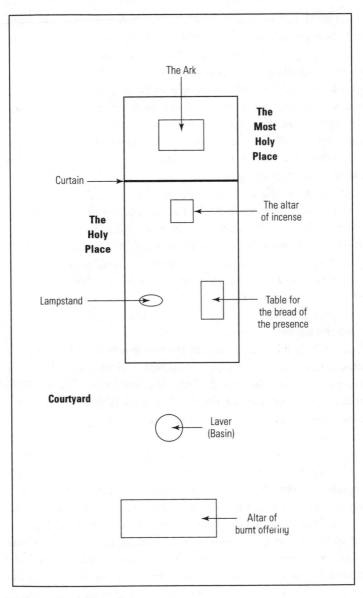

Figure 19. The tabernacle

The sacrificial system is designed to deal with this problem. Sacrifices are offered in the tabernacle every day for the sin of the people. There is also an annual Day of Atonement (Leviticus 16), on which the high priest is to take two goats. He is to kill the first goat as a sin offering for the people and then sprinkle its blood on the atonement cover in the Most Holy Place. The Israelites deserve to die for their sin, but God provides the goat as a substitute, to die in their place. The blood speaks of the life that has been laid down for sin: 'For the life of a creature is in the blood, and I have given it to you to make atonement for yourselves on the altar; it is the blood that makes atonement for one's life' (Leviticus 17:11). The people can live because the animal has died. The results of that atonement (reconciliation, or at-one-ment, with God) are seen in what happens to the second goat. The sins of the people are confessed over it and then it is driven far away. God has dealt with sin and can thus continue to live with the Israelites.

A better sacrifice

God does live with his people in the tabernacle, but they dare not get too close. Only one man, once a year, can enter the Most Holy Place: the high priest on the Day of Atonement. The sacrifices enable some measure of relationship with God, but it is not a close one. They never fully deal with sin. They point beyond themselves to the perfect sacrifice that Christ would offer through his death on the cross. His death deals with sin once and for all; it never needs to be repeated. It opens up the way into God's presence 'beyond the veil' to all who trust in him. When he dies, the curtain in the temple (the permanent structure in Jerusalem, which later replaced the tabernacle) is torn in two by God (Mark 15:58). The symbolism is powerful. The door to God's presence is now wide open for all who will go in: ' . . . we have confidence to enter the Most Holy Place by the blood of Jesus, by a new and living way opened for us through the curtain' (Hebrews 10:19–20).

Right through the Bible, God saves through providing a substitute to die in the place of others. The different sacrifices in the Old Testament point ahead to the perfect sacrifice offered by Jesus when he died on the cross.

- A sacrifice for a man: Abraham and Isaac (Genesis 22)
- A sacrifice for a family: the Passover (Exodus 12)
- A sacrifice for a nation: the Day of Atonement (Leviticus 16)
- A sacrifice for the world: the death of Jesus (John 1:29; 1 John 2:2)

Figure 20. Sacrifice in the Bible

Bible study

Exodus 19:1–13; 20:1–17

19:1–13
What does this passage teach us about God?

How does it challenge the way we often think about him?

How should we relate to such a God?

What has God already done for the Israelites (see also 20:2)?

What does he promise to do in the future?

How do these promises relate to the promises he made to Abraham (Genesis 12:1–3)?

What must the people do? Is that possible?

How can God's promises be fulfilled?

20:1–17
How many of the Ten Commandments have you obeyed?

Why should we want to obey them as Christians?

Which do you find especially hard to obey?

What practical steps can you take to ensure that you obey those commands more?

God's place

The promise

'To your offspring I will give this land.'
(Genesis 12:7)

The partial fulfilment

Once the law had been given and the tabernacle established, the Israelites were God's people under God's rule, enjoying the blessing that came from his presence with them. But they were a people without a land. The next section of the history of the Bible is focused on their entrance to the promised land.

Numbers: disobedience and delay

After their detour to meet God on Mount Sinai, we find the Israelites ready to set out on their journey to Canaan at the beginning of the book of Numbers. The rabble from Egypt is now organized and is beginning to look like an impressive army. And when they set out, God marches in front of them in a pillar of cloud (Numbers 10:11–12). Surely nothing can go wrong now. We expect them to reach their destination in a matter of months, but it actually takes them forty years.

Within hours of setting out, they start grumbling about the quality of the food and about the leadership of Moses. The final straw comes when some scouts return from a trip to Canaan. They report that it is a land flowing 'with milk and honey' and that 'the people who live there are powerful, and the cities are fortified and very large' (Numbers 13:27–28). The people are terrified and refuse to enter the land, convinced that they will be destroyed. 'We'd be better off back in Egypt,' they say (see 14:3). Their response shows not only terrible ingratitude but also unbelief. Two of the scouts, Joshua and Caleb, plead with them to trust in God: ' . . . do not be afraid of the people of the land, because we will swallow them up. Their protection is gone, but the LORD is with us' (14:9). But, despite all the evidence of God's power that they had seen when he delivered them from Egypt, the people will not trust him. God responds by judging them. All of that generation, except for Caleb and Joshua, will die before they enter the land.

The apostle Paul tells us that their fate is a warning to us: 'these things occurred as examples to keep us from setting our hearts on evil things as they did' (1 Corinthians 10:6). If we have faith in Christ, we too have been set free from slavery (to sin, not to Egypt) by a Passover sacrifice (of Jesus, not of a lamb), and have been set on a journey to the promised land (heaven, not Canaan). We must make sure that we do not fall because of sin and unbelief, but that we keep trusting God until we reach the destination.

Deuteronomy: blessings and curses

The book of Deuteronomy takes us to the very brink of the land, on the plains of Moab by the river Jordan. Moses speaks to the people one final time before he dies. Addressing the next generation, he pleads with them, 'Don't blow it like we did.' He reminds them of what God has said and done in the past, and urges them, 'Now it's up to you to believe and obey; to live in the light of the gospel when you enter the land.' 'For you are a people holy to the LORD your God. The LORD your God has chosen you out of all the peoples on the face of the earth to be his people, his treasured possession ... And now, O Israel, What does the LORD your God ask of you but to fear the LORD your God, to walk in all his ways, to love him, to serve the LORD your God with all your heart and with all your soul, and to observe the LORD's commands ...?' (Deuteronomy 7:6; 10:12–13).

The stakes are high. On the one hand, if they obey, they will be blessed: 'If you fully obey the LORD your God and carefully follow all his commands that I give you today, the LORD your God will set you high above all the nations on earth' (28:1). Moses then gives a long list of blessings they can expect. But, on the other hand, ' ... if you do not obey the LORD your God and do not carefully follow all his commands ... all these curses will come upon you and overtake you . . .' (28:15). The list that follows is dreadful and culminates in a promise that God will evict them from the promised land: 'You will be uprooted from the land you are entering to possess. Then the LORD will scatter you among all nations, from one end of the earth to the other' (28:63–64).

So a big question mark hovers over the Israelites as they prepare to enter the land. How will they live when they get there? Will they keep the covenant and prosper? Or will they disobey and be expelled from the land?

Joshua: the conquest

When Moses dies he is succeeded by Joshua, and it is under him that the Israelites finally enter Canaan. They defeat the former inhabitants and take possession of the land for themselves. As they do so, they are left in no doubt that the conquest is not a victory they can claim for themselves. They are powerless, but God is mighty. That is seen most clearly in the siege of Jericho, when God causes the walls to collapse before them.

Our modern ears are disturbed by God's command to the Israelites to destroy the former inhabitants of the land. It sounds like ethnic cleansing. But God is not motivated by racial prejudice. Moses said that 'it is on account of the wickedness of these nations that the LORD is going to drive them out before you' (Deuteronomy 9:4–5). In his perfect righteousness, God is provoked by the awful wickedness of the Canaanites, which includes idolatry, immorality and child sacrifice. He knows that his holy people will be corrupted by such evil if it is allowed to stay in the land. That is exactly what eventually happens. The Israelites fail to obey the command to destroy the Canaanites fully, and they remain a corrupting influence on them for many years.

The book of Joshua moves towards its conclusion on a high note: ' . . . the LORD gave Israel all the land he had sworn to give their forefathers, and they took possession of it and settled there. The LORD gave them rest on every side, just as he had sworn to their forefathers . . . Not one of all the LORD's good promises to the house of Israel failed; every one was fulfilled' (Joshua 21:43–45). It is a time of fulfilment. God's people are in God's place under God's rule and are enjoying his blessing ('rest').

But a note of caution is also struck as the book ends. Joshua gives a farewell sermon to his people, rather as Moses had done in Deuteronomy. He urges them to fear God and to obey his law. And he warns them that, if they disobey, they will be expelled from the land: '... if you turn away and ally yourselves with the survivors of these nations that remain among you ... then you may be sure that the LORD your God will no longer drive out these nations before you. Instead, they will become snares and traps for you ... until you perish from this good land, which the LORD your God has given you' (23:12–13). The question mark remains. Will the people obey God? How long will they be able to stay in the land?

God's king

The promise
Abraham was not explicitly told that God's people would be ruled by a king, but it is hinted at and clearly stated elsewhere.

'... he will crush your head.'
(Genesis 3:15)

God tells the snake that he will be defeated by one of Eve's offspring. The rest of the Bible can be seen as a 'search for the serpent-crusher'. Who will this great conqueror be?

'The sceptre will not depart from Judah,
    nor the ruler's staff from between his feet,
until he comes to whom it belongs
    and the obedience of the nations is his.'
(Genesis 49:10)

Jacob blesses his son Jacob before he dies and tells him that one of his descendants will rule over all nations for ever.

> 'When you enter the land the LORD your God is giving you and have taken possession of it and settled in it, and you say, "Let us set a king over us like all the nations around us," be sure to appoint over you the king the LORD your God chooses . . .
> 'When he takes the throne of his kingdom, he is to write for himself on a scroll a copy of this law . . . It is to be with him, and he is to read it all the days of his life so that he may learn to revere the LORD his God and follow carefully all the words of this law . . .'
> (Deuteronomy 17:14–20)

Before the Israelites entered the land, God planned that they should be governed by a king. This king was not to be an authority separate from God, but would rule under God, submitting to him and his law. So the promise of a king is really a subset of the promise of God's rule and blessing. God rules in his kingdom by means of a king.

The partial fulfilment

Judges: a cycle of sin and grace
Judges tells the story of the Israelites in the promised land in the years after the death of Joshua. It makes depressing reading. The people do not heed the warnings of Moses and Joshua, but rebel against God's rule. The same cycle is repeated again and again throughout the book. The Israelites turn from God and serve other gods. God responds by judging them and allowing them to be defeated by their enemies. They then cry out to the LORD for help, and he responds by raising up a 'judge' or 'ruler'. These judges defeat the enemies in the power of God's Spirit and restore peace to the land, but it never lasts for long. The people soon

turn away from God again, and the cycle is repeated (see e.g. 3:7–12).

Why should God bother to save the Israelites after their continued disobedience? The judges are a great sign of God's grace. But they are not an adequate solution to the problems of Israel. They are a fairly motley crowd who are certainly not models of godly living. Jephthah kills his own daughter, and Samson is a womanizing thug. We miss the point if we try to turn them into great heroes for the Sunday-school class to emulate. While praising God for the deliverance he achieved through them, we should be longing for a better leader, who will bring about a lasting solution to the problem of Israel's sin; we should be longing for a king. Judges hints that everything would be so much better if a king were appointed. It ends with some words which appear four times in the book: 'In those days Israel had no king; everyone did as he saw fit' (21:25).

1 Samuel: a false start

Samuel is the greatest judge to rule Israel. He serves God all through his life, but, when he grows old, he appoints his wicked sons as judges in his place. The elders of Israel come to him and demand that he appoint a king to rule them, 'such as all the other nations have' (1 Samuel 8:5). God is angry with them for their request, not because they want a king but because of their motivation in asking for one. They want a king *instead of* God rather than a king *under* God. In their desire to be like the other nations they are rejecting God's kingship over them, which made them unique. The want a monarchy instead of a theocracy.

Despite the sinfulness of their request, God gives them what they ask for and Saul is anointed as king. But the people are not blessed during his reign, because he persistently disobeys God. As a result, God delivers his verdict on him through Samuel: 'Because you have rejected the word of the LORD, he has rejected you as king' (1 Samuel 15:23).

The focus is now on David, who has already been anointed as

Saul's heir. God's presence with him is demonstrated very early on when he defeats Goliath, the mighty Philistine champion, single-handed (1 Samuel 17). But, just as Jesus (David's descendant) is to discover many years later, being the Lord's anointed does not guarantee a smooth passage through life. Saul is jealous of David and tries to kill him. He is forced to live as a fugitive until Saul dies in a battle against the Philistines. David then becomes king in his place.

2 Samuel: the reign of David

At last Israel has the kind of king God wants: 'a man after his own heart' (1 Samuel 13:14). David is not perfect: his lust leads him to commit adultery with Bathsheba and then to order the murder of her husband. But, for most of his life, he seeks to be faithful to God, and so God blesses him and the people through him. At first, only his own tribe of Judah acknowledges him as their king, but after a few years all Israel follows. He immediately establishes Jerusalem as his capital city and secures peace in the land. The ark, symbolizing God's presence and rule, is brought into the city. David rules, not independently of God, but under him. Jerusalem is not just the city of David; it is the city of God. Israel has never before enjoyed such peace and prosperity in its history. But still the time of fulfilment has not come. David is not the serpent-crusher of Genesis 3:15, or the great ruler from the tribe of Judah promised in Genesis 49:10. There is still one greater to come, as God makes clear through the prophet Nathan.

God underlines the covenant promises he made to Abraham in Genesis 12 (2 Samuel 7:9–11) and then prophesies a future king who is far greater even than David (verses 11–16). It becomes clear that the future of the covenant depends on this future king. God will fulfil his promises through this great son of David, who is also a son of God:

'When your days are over and you rest with your fathers, I will raise up your offspring to succeed you, who will come from your own body ... I will be his father, and he shall be my son. When he does wrong, I will punish him with the rod of men, with floggings inflicted by men. But my love will never be taken away from him, as I took it away from Saul, whom I removed from before you. Your house and your kingdom shall endure for ever before me; your throne shall be established for ever.'

(2 Samuel 7:12–16)

One promise does not seem to fit with the others: 'When he does wrong, I will punish him.' That suggests a normal human being, whereas the others suggest someone much greater. How can we hold these two sides together? The answer is that, like many Old Testament prophecies, this prophecy is fulfilled at more than one level. As we shall soon see, it is partially fulfilled by the great king Solomon, who was to build the temple. But it is finally fulfilled only by the Lord Jesus, 'great David's greater son', the one whose reign puts Solomon's into the shadows (see Luke 11:31).

From 2 Samuel 7 onwards in the Bible, we are waiting for the arrival of God's king, the son of David. The kingdom of God must be established by him, the 'Messiah' or 'Christ'. 'Messiah' is from a Hebrew word which means 'anointed one'. 'Christ' is from the Greek translation, *Christos*.

1 Kings 1 – 11: Solomon and the golden age
Solomon succeeds David as king and rules wisely. He brings security and prosperity to the land. And the temple is built during his reign, providing a permanent symbolic dwelling-place for God. The nation has never had it so good. We have reached the pinnacle of the Old Testament. It looks now as if all the promises of God have been fulfilled and the kingdom of God has come. At the dedication of the temple Solomon prays, 'Praise be to the LORD, who has given rest to his people Israel just as he promised. Not one word has failed of all the good promises he gave through

his servant Moses' (1 Kings 8:56). God's people are in God's place under God's rule and are enjoying God's blessing.

They are *God's people*: 'The people of Judah and Israel were as numerous as the sand on the seashore' (4:20), just as God had promised (Genesis 32:12).

They are *in God's place*: 'Solomon ruled over all the kingdoms from the River to the land of the Philistines, as far as the border of Egypt' (4:21). The whole land was under his control, as God had said at the time of Moses (Exodus 23:31).

They *enjoy God's rule and blessing*: The ark, the symbol of God's rule, is in the temple (8:21). They are blessed: 'During Solomon's lifetime Judah and Israel, from to Dan to Beersheba, lived in safety, each man under his own vine and fig-tree' (4:25). And they are a blessing to the nations; it was always God's plan that all nations would be blessed through his people. There are signs that this is happening during Solomon's reign – for example, in the

The kingdom of God	The pattern of the kingdom	The perished kingdom	The promised kingdom	The partial kingdom
God's people	Adam and Eve	No-one	Abraham's descendants	The Israelites
God's place	The garden	Banished	Canaan	Canaan (and Jerusalem and temple)
God's rule and blessing	God's word; perfect relation-ships	Disobedi-ence and curse	Blessing to Israel and the nations	The law and the king

Figure 21. The partial kingdom

visit of the Queen of Sheba, who praises God for the king's
wisdom and benefits from his prosperity (1 Kings 10:1–13).

Everything looks so good, but it is not to last. Solomon marries
many foreign wives and begins to worship their gods (1 Kings 11).
For David's sake, God delays his judgment until Solomon dies,
but then he causes civil war to break out and the kingdom begins
to disintegrate.

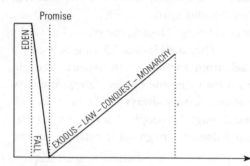

Figure 22. The story so far: the monarchy

1 Kings 12 – 2 Kings 25: disobedience, division and decline
Soon after Solomon's son, Rehoboam, comes to the throne, the
ten northern and eastern tribes rebel against him and set up their
own kingdom under Jeroboam. Israel has been united for 120
years under Saul, David and Solomon, but now it is divided. The
northern kingdom is, confusingly, called Israel, with its capital city
in Shechem and, later, in Samaria. The southern kingdom, Judah,
has Jerusalem as its capital. There are occasionally good kings in
both kingdoms, but the general direction of their history is
downwards.

The decline is obvious in the north from the very beginning.
Jeroboam is concerned that his people will continue to want to go
to Jerusalem in the southern kingdom to meet with God at the
temple. He establishes two alternative shrines, at Bethel and Dan,
and puts a golden calf in each, saying, 'Here are your gods, O

There are three wisdom books in the Old Testament: Proverbs, Ecclesiastes and Job. Because much of the first two is attributed to Solomon, it seems appropriate to mention them at this point.

- Proverbs is a collection of pithy sayings that point in detail to the wise way to live.
- Ecclesiastes examines what life looks like if God is removed: 'Everything is meaningless' (1:2).
- Job describes the suffering of an innocent man. Sometimes wisdom accepts that there are no easy answers (such as those offered by Job's unhelpful comforters), and simply trusts in God.

The wisdom books do not belong at any one chronological point in the history of God's unfolding work of salvation. They speak to all ages about how life should be lived in his kingdom.

- The beginning of wisdom is the fear of the Lord (Proverbs 1:7; Job 28:28).
- Jesus is the fulfilment of wisdom. As David's greater son, he is wiser even than Solomon (1 Kings 3; Matthew 12:42). He is himself 'the wisdom of God' (1 Corinthians 1:24), and we can become wise in him (1 Corinthians 1:30). The wise person is the one who hears and obeys his word (Matthew 7:24).

Figure 23. The wisdom books: life in the kingdom

Israel, who brought you up out of Egypt' (1 Kings 12:28). Aaron had said exactly the same after he and the people had made another golden calf while Moses was on Mount Sinai receiving the law from God (Exodus 32:4). This idolatrous worship is the besetting sin of Israel throughout its existence. It is only a matter of time before God acts in judgment.

The end comes in 722 BC, 200 years after the kingdoms divided. The Assyrians attack Samaria and destroy it. There is no doubt why this happens: 'All this took place because the Israelites had sinned against the LORD their God, who had brought them out of

Egypt' (2 Kings 17:7). The ten northern tribes will never have a separate existence again. Their descendants are the Samaritans, so despised by the Jews at the time of Christ.

The southern kingdom of Judah fares no better. Its sad story of decline is told in the second half of 2 Kings and also in 2 Chronicles. Even though they have the temple in their midst, the people turn to other gods. There are periods when they are more obedient to God, in particular under King Josiah, who promotes religious reform after he finds a copy of the law in the temple. But the change does not go far enough, or deep enough, to deflect God's anger. The people have broken his covenant and they must be punished. God had warned them before they entered the land that they would not be allowed to stay if they disobeyed. He keeps his word when the Babylonians defeat Judah in 597 BC and take some of its inhabitants into exile. The judgment is extended soon afterwards, in 586 BC, when the city and its temple are destroyed and many more are taken to Babylon.

No wonder they sing, 'By the rivers of Babylon we sat and wept when we remembered Zion' (Psalm 137:1). They have lost so much. The golden age they had enjoyed under Solomon is nothing but a distant memory; the partial kingdom has been dismantled. There is very little evidence that they are God's people; they are not in God's place, but in exile; and they face the curse of God's judgment rather than his blessing. It is as if the fall has happened all over again. God had warned them before they entered the promised land that they would be evicted if they did not obey him (Deuteronomy 28:25, 63–64; Joshua 23:12–13). But they have rejected his rule and, as a result, they are banished from his presence.

The partial kingdom is dismantled
It is all so sad, but it is not the end of the Bible's story. God's work among the Israelites was never intended to be the final fulfilment of his gospel promises. Within the context of the Bible as a whole,

the history of Israel serves as a model. That model of Concorde you made as a child may have been very impressive, but it was not the real thing. It pointed to something bigger and better: the aeroplane itself. In a similar way, the partial kingdom is just a shadow of the perfect kingdom that God will establish through Jesus Christ. It points beyond itself to him. Yes, it was great for the Israelites to be rescued from slavery to the Egyptians, but that rescue is just a pale shadow of the perfect redemption achieved by Jesus on the cross (John 1:29; 1 Corinthians 5:7). Yes, it was wonderful for the Israelites to have God's presence in their midst in the tabernacle and the temple, but those structures were just shadows of the one in whom the presence of God was perfectly manifest: 'The Word became flesh and made his dwelling [or "tabernacled"] among us' (John 1:14). And yes, David and Solomon were great kings, but Jesus is far greater (Mark 12:35–37; Luke 11:31). God may have rejected his model, but he has not forgotten his promises. As we shall see in the next chapter, it is the role of the prophets to explain that great truth. They stress that the decline of Israel and Judah is not out of God's control. He is at work dismantling the model because of the sin of his people. But that is not the end. God will never rebuild the model again, but he will establish the real thing in and through Jesus.

Bible study

2 Samuel 7:1–17

What does David want to build (verses 1–2)?

But what does God want to build (verses 4–7)?

What has God already done for David (verse 8)?

What does he promise to do in the future (verses 9–11)?

How do these promises echo the promises made to Abraham in Genesis 12:1–3?

What does God promise concerning the coming king (verses 12–16)?

How does Jesus fulfil these promises? (See Matthew 1:1; Mark 12:35–37; John 2:18–22; Acts 2:24–36; Romans 1:1–4.)

What implications does this have for
• our understanding of Jesus?

• our relationship with Jesus?

5

The prophesied kingdom

God's mouthpiece

Moses was fearful when God told him to speak to the Israelites in his name, so he was allowed to take Aaron with him as his spokesman. God said, 'He will speak to the people for you, and it will be as if he were your mouth and as if you were God to him ... I have made you like God to Pharaoh; and your brother Aaron will be your prophet. You are to say everything I command you, and your brother Aaron is to tell Pharaoh to let the Israelites go out of his country' (Exodus 4:16; 7:1–2). Those words provide us with a good definition of the role of a prophet. Aaron was Moses' 'prophet', passing on to the people the words Moses first gave him. So God's prophets are his mouthpieces, proclaiming his word to others. Peter writes in the New Testament, 'Prophecy never had its origin in the will of man, but men spoke from God as they were carried along by the Holy Spirit' (2 Peter 1:21). That is exactly the claim they made for themselves. For example, the words of the prophet Jeremiah begin with the introduction: 'The word of the LORD came to me ...' (Jeremiah 1:4).

Covenant enforcers

Moses was the definitive prophet, through whom God revealed his law at Sinai. All future generations were to live in the light of that covenant. If they wished to remain in the land and enjoy God's blessing there, they had to obey his law. If they did not, they would face his judgment and would ultimately be exiled from the land. The role of the prophets who succeeded Moses was to enforce the covenant, urging the people to obey it and reminding them of the blessings that followed obedience and the curses that followed disobedience.

The first great prophets after Moses are Elijah and Elisha, who are both active in the northern kingdom of Israel in the ninth century BC. Much of their ministry involves public confrontations with the kings of Israel. They call the kings to live according to God's law and to repent of their idolatry and lack of trust in him. Israel's spiritual state is very low during their ministry. There is widespread apostasy under King Ahab. Many of God's prophets are killed and Baal is worshipped throughout the land. Elijah challenges the prophets of Baal to a public contest on Mount Carmel. This results in a resounding victory for the one true God. But, even then, most of the people do not worship him. A dejected Elijah speaks to God: 'The Israelites have rejected your covenant, broken down your altars, and put your prophets to death with the sword. I am the only one left' (1 Kings 19:10). God reassures him: 'I reserve seven thousand in Israel – all whose knees have not bowed down to Baal' (19:18). Seven thousand is better than one, but it is still a very small proportion of the nation. And yet, despite such abundant wickedness, Elijah and Elisha still seem to think that there is time for the people to return to the Lord before his judgment comes. As time passes, however, the prophets come to see that judgment is inevitable.

The writing prophets

From the eighth century BC onwards, the prophets begin to write down their oracles, and many have been preserved for us in the

Bible. Some, like Amos and Hosea, are active in the northern kingdom in the few decades leading to its destruction by the Assyrians in 922 BC. The rest prophesy in Judah: some, like Isaiah, Micah and Jeremiah, in the period leading up to the exile in 597/586 BC; others, such as Ezekiel and Daniel, during the exile; and some, like Haggai, Zechariah and Malachi, after the return from exile (Figure 24).

Northern kingdom	Eighth century BC	Amos, Hosea
Southern kingdom	Eighth century BC	Isaiah, Micah
	Seventh century BC (incl. exile)	Jeremiah, Ezekiel, Daniel
	Sixth century BC (post-exilic)	Haggai, Zechariah, Malachi

Figure 24. Dates of some of the prophets

There are seventeen prophetic books in the Bible. They are often referred to as 'major prophets' (Isaiah, Jeremiah and Ezekiel) and 'minor prophets' (the rest). The minor prophets are not less important than the others; they are so called because their books are shorter. Each group has two dominant themes: judgment and hope, both of which are based on God's covenant.

Judgment

God's judgment is hardly mentioned in some churches. Their ministers clearly do not preach from the prophets very often. By contrast, long sections in the prophetic books are devoted to exposing the people's sin and announcing God's judgment against it. We must not think of the prophets as only predicting what God will do through Christ in the future. They first spoke to their own day; they were 'forthtellers', not just 'foretellers', and their main message was one of judgment (Figure 25).

Judgment on the nations (1:3 – 2:3)
As the creator of the whole world, God is concerned not just with the behaviour of his own people; he will bring everyone to account.

Judgment on Judah (2:4–5)
God's own people are especially culpable because they have disobeyed his covenant:

'Because they have rejected the law of the LORD
  and have not kept his decrees,
because they have been led astray by false gods,
  the gods their ancestors followed,
I will send fire upon Judah
  that will consume the fortresses of Jerusalem.'

Judgment on Israel (2:6ff.)
Having condemned her neighbours, God's word through Amos now turns on his own nation. The Israelites have assumed that they would be immune from judgment because they are God's people, but that fact has made their sin even worse. He had done so much for them over the years: 'I brought you up out of Egypt . . . I also raised up prophets from among your sons' but 'you commanded the prophets not to prophesy' (2:10–12). Amos exposes their sin in every area of life. He is concerned with their social behaviour (their greed and injustice) as much as with their religious life. As the creator, God is lord of all areas of life and expects to be obeyed in everything. A 'day of the LORD' is coming when they will be brought to account. It will not be the day they have been expecting, when their enemies will be destroyed. No, they themselves will face God's anger (5:18).

Figure 25. Judgment in the book of Amos

The people of both Israel and Judah are complacent and do not take the warnings seriously. But their complacency is shattered when the Assyrians defeat Israel in 722 BC and the Babylonians destroy Jerusalem and take the people of Judah into exile in 597 and 586 BC. The prophets stress that these events are not historical accidents; they are acts of God's judgment in fulfilment of his word to them when he inaugurated the covenant at the time of Moses.

A friend of mine has explained it like this. Jamie is a young boy who has just been given some new shoes. It is a rainy day, and his mother knows that he likes splashing in puddles, so she warns him, 'If you go into those puddles, you'll be sent to your room when you get home.' But he goes straight into the first one he sees. His mother tells him off: 'If you keep on doing that, you'll go straight to your room when you get home.' But Jamie splashes in the next puddle he passes, and the one after that as well. So, when he gets home, he is sent up to his room, where he begins to bawl with tears. His mother speaks to him from outside the door: 'Jamie, it's your own fault. I told you very clearly that, if you carried on splashing in the puddles, you'd be sent to your room. You kept doing it and that's why you're there now.'

The parallels with the Israelites are obvious. They are given a very clear warning, through Moses and Joshua, even before they enter the land: 'If you turn away from God, you will be judged and sent into exile.' They do disobey, so God, through the prophets, reminds them, 'If you continue to live like this, God will judge you.' God is patient with them for many years, but still they do not repent, so, in the end, judgment comes. And then God speaks again, through prophets like Ezekiel at the time of the exile, explaining what is happening to them: 'God is punishing you, just as he said he would.' They are not to think that Jerusalem has been defeated because God is less powerful than the Babylonian gods. He is still in control. He has been at work through the Babylonians, carrying out the judgment he has promised.

God has not changed. He is still the God of infinite love, but he is also a holy God who hates what is evil and gets angry when he sees it. His judgment on his people in the Old Testament should warn us against being complacent, as they were. It is a foretaste of a far more terrible judgment to come at the end of time. On that day we shall have to stand before God and be held to account for how we have lived on earth (Revelation 20:11–15). Our only hope will be to trust in Christ and his death for us.

Hope

To be faithful to his word, God has to judge his people. But that same word demands that the judgment will not be the end of his dealings with them. There is a conditional element to God's promises; he has made it clear through Moses that they will forgo his blessing if they disobey. But there is also an unconditional element to them; his promise to Abraham is a guaranteed commitment:

> 'I will make you into a great nation
>   and I will bless you;
> I will make your name great,
>   and you will be a blessing.
> I will bless those who bless you,
>   and whoever curses you I will curse;
> and all peoples on earth
>   will be blessed through you.'
> (Genesis 12:1–3)

So God's covenant, which is the basis of the prophets' message of judgment, is also the basis of the other major theme of their books: hope.

While their history proclaimed the failure of Israel, the prophets proclaim the future of Israel. They speak of good times ahead in terms of action replay: 'Do you remember what it was like in the good old days under Moses, David and Solomon?' they ask. 'Well, it will be like that again in the future, only much better.' There will be a new exodus, a new covenant, a new nation, a new Jerusalem, a new temple, a new king, and even a new creation. God will not rebuild the model, the partial kingdom, but he will establish that to which it pointed, the real thing, the perfect kingdom: God's people in God's place, under God's rule and enjoying his blessing. The prophets spoke of the ultimate fulfilment of all three of those kingdom promises.

God's people

The remnant
Although God will bring terrible judgment on his people, he will not destroy them completely. A remnant will be preserved, out of whom God will create a new nation:

> In that day the remnant of Israel,
>   the survivors of the house of Jacob,
> will no longer rely on him
>   who struck them down
> but will truly rely on the LORD,
>   the Holy One of Israel.
> A remnant will return, a remnant of Jacob
>   will return to the Mighty God.
> (Isaiah 10:20–21)

Isaiah is even instructed to call one of his sons 'Shear-Jashub' (which means 'a remnant will return') to underline the message.

A new exodus
The plight of the people of Judah in exile in Babylon is similar to that of the Israelites when they were slaves in Egypt. As God rescued them then, so he will rescue them again. There will be a new exodus: 'The days are coming … when men will no longer say, "As surely as the LORD lives, who brought the Israelites up out of Egypt," but they will say, "As surely as the LORD lives, who brought the Israelites up out of the land of the north and out of all the countries where he had banished them." For I will restore them to the land I gave to their forefathers' (Jeremiah 16:14–15).

The servant

Isaiah stresses that the new exodus will be achieved by a mysterious figure he calls 'the servant'. Sometimes the servant is identified as the nation of Israel (e.g. 44:1–2). But in other passages it is clear that he is an individual who will be used by God to rescue the remnant of Israel (e.g. 49:5–6; 52:13 – 53:12). He will achieve this rescue by his death. God uses what is known as the 'prophetic perfect' tense, speaking of a future event as if it had already taken place, because it is so certain:

'. . . he was pierced for our transgressions,
    he was crushed for our iniquities;
the punishment that brought us peace was upon him,
    and by his wounds we are healed.
We all, like sheep, have gone astray,
    each of us has turned to his own way;
and the LORD has laid on him
    the iniquity of us all.'
(Isaiah 53:5–6)

This individual is both the true Israel and the one who dies for the remnant of Israel, so that God's people can be rescued from their sin. He will face their punishment, exile from God, in their place, so that they can be forgiven and a new Israel constituted. This prophecy was to be fulfilled when Jesus died on the cross. He had said of himself: '. . . even the Son of Man did not come to be served, but to serve, and to give his life as a ransom for many' (Mark 10:45).

The inclusion of the nations

The servant's role extends beyond Israel. Just as Israel was to be a kingdom of priests, channelling the blessings of his rule to the nations (Exodus 19:6), God says to the servant,

'It is too small a thing for you to be my servant
    to restore the tribes of Jacob

and bring back those of Israel I have kept.
I will also make you a light for the Gentiles,
that you may bring my salvation to the ends of the earth.'
(Isaiah 49:6)

The promise to Abraham of blessing to the nations will be fulfilled. Men and women from all peoples will benefit when God acts to save Israel (Isaiah 60:1–3).

God's place

New temple

The book of Ezekiel begins with a vision of the glory of God leaving the temple in Jerusalem. He is acting in judgment and withdrawing from his people. The building is now nothing but an empty shell and it is only a matter of time before it is destroyed by the Babylonians. But the book ends with great hope. Ezekiel has another vision of a new temple, more magnificent than the first (chapters 40 – 48), and he sees God entering it. A river flows out from this new temple, giving life to the world.

The new creation

Ezekiel's vision of a new temple is so magnificent that it cannot refer simply to one building on earth. It is a symbol of a new creation. God's plan of salvation is not limited to the Israelites, or even to human beings of all nations. The creator of everything is determined to undo completely the effects of the fall and to renew the whole world. The new Jerusalem in which his people will live is not a city located somewhere on earth; it is a new creation. God says,

'Behold, I will create
new heavens and a new earth.
The former things will not be remembered,
nor will they come to mind.

But be glad and rejoice for ever
   in what I will create,
for I will create Jerusalem to be a delight
   and its people a joy.'
(Isaiah 65:17–18)

The book of Psalms is a collection of hymns and prayers used by the people of Israel in their worship. It does not belong to any one period in Israel's history, the individual psalms having been written over a long period of time, many of them by King David. The book has been described as 'the little Bible', as all the Bible's themes are found within it. Let us notice three themes.

Praise
Like the rest of the Bible, the Psalms are focused above all on God. He is the great king of all the earth and of his people Israel. His people praise him for the power, holiness and justice of his rule and for his compassion in saving them.

   Come, let us sing for joy to the LORD;
      let us shout aloud to the Rock of our salvation.
   Let us come before him with thanksgiving
      and extol him with music and song.

   For the LORD is the great God,
      the great King above all gods.
   (Psalm 95:1–3)

See also Psalms 100; 121; 145.

Prophecy
The book of Psalms is quoted in the New Testament more than any other Old Testament book. Some of the Psalms clearly point forward to

---

Figure 26. The Psalms: 'The LORD is king' (Psalm 10:16)

the Lord Jesus. He will be enthroned above the universe as God's eternal king:

> Your throne, O God, will last for ever and ever;
>> a sceptre of justice will be the sceptre of your kingdom.
> You love righteousness and hate wickedness;
>> therefore God, your God, has set you above your companions
>> by anointing you with the oil of joy.
> (Psalm 45:6–7)

But his reign will be established only through suffering. He will know suffering so intense that he will cry out, 'My God, my God, why have you forsaken me?' (Psalm 22:1). See also Psalms 2; 89:19–29; 110.

Personal experience

In the Psalms we find not just God speaking to his people, but his people speaking to him. We are given an insight into the believer's heart. The experience of faith in God the King is laid bare before us in all its variety. The mood varies from great certainty and joy to doubt and depression. The Christian believer can expect to experience similar feelings: the King has not changed. The words of the psalmist can become our own:

> How long, O LORD? Will you forget me for ever?
>> How long will you hide your face from me?
> (13:1)

> The LORD is my light and my salvation – whom shall I fear?
> (27:1)

> How lovely is your dwelling-place,
>> O LORD Almighty!
> My soul yearns, even faints,
>> for the courts of the LORD.
> (84:1)

See also Psalms 23; 42; 73.

Figure 26 (*cont.*). The Psalms: 'The LORD is king' (Psalm 10:16)

God's rule and blessing

The new covenant

> ' "The time is coming," declares the LORD,
>   "when I will make a new covenant
> with the house of Israel
>   and with the house of Judah." '
> (Jeremiah 31:31)

This covenant will not be a completely new start. God is not abandoning the promises he has made in the past. But how can he fulfil those promises to bless his people? In his faithfulness, he must do so if he is to keep his word. And yet he is also bound to punish the Israelites if they disobey him. So how can he bless them, given their continued sinfulness? The new covenant will make this possible. It will be unbreakable. God will find a way of dealing with sin, so that all his people will be forgiven and know God intimately. He will change them from within: 'I will put my law in their minds and write it on their hearts' (31:33). Ezekiel and Joel make it clear that this is a promise of the presence of God's Holy Spirit in the lives of all God's people (Ezekiel 36:26–27; Joel 2:28–32). This new covenant was to be inaugurated by Jesus' death. When he took the cup at the last supper he said, 'This cup is the new covenant in my blood, which is poured out for you' (Luke 22:20).

The new king

As God had ruled through a king in the days of the old covenant, so he would do again in the new-covenant era. The prophets build on the promise God had made to David (in 2 Samuel 7:12–16) that an eternal, universal king would come from his line. The salvation of God's people and the fulfilment of all God's promises depend on the coming of this anointed one (or 'Christ', 'Messiah'), the son of David:

For to us a child is born,
    to us a son is given . . .
Of the increase of his government and peace
    there will be no end.
He will reign on David's throne
    and over his kingdom,
establishing and upholding it
    with justice and righteousness
    from that time on and for ever.
(Isaiah 9:6–7)

Daniel says he is 'like a son of man'. In his vision, this son of man 'was given authority, glory and sovereign power; all peoples, nations and men of every language worshipped him' (Daniel 7:13–14). Such passages make it clear that he is no ordinary king. It is only when Christ comes that believers begin to see the implication of many of the prophecies about him. His reign is God's reign because he is God. Jesus himself points out the implication of Psalm 110:1:

The LORD says to my Lord:
    'Sit at my right hand
until I make your enemies
    a footstool for your feet.'

The psalmist, David, refers to another ruler as 'my Lord'. He is no mere son of David; he must also be the Son of God (Mark 12:35–37).

Great blessing
The time of fulfilment will be marked by great blessing for the whole world. With God's rule established, everything falls into place once more. There is a return to the blessings of Eden; peace and prosperity will abound.

... the reaper will be overtaken by the ploughman
   and the planter by the one treading grapes.
New wine will drip from the mountains
   and flow from all the hills.
(Amos 9:13–14)

The wolf will live with the lamb,
   the leopard will lie down with the goat,
the calf and the lion and the yearling together;
   and a little child will lead them.
(Isaiah 11:6)

The return from exile

In 538 BC, just six decades after the exile had begun, it looks as if the prophecies of hope are about to be fulfilled. Cyrus of Persia defeats the Babylonians and issues an edict that allows the exiles to return and rebuild their temple. But the restoration of the nation is not the triumphant success that the prophets had promised. Only a small number make the journey back to their homeland. They face great opposition when they do so, but eventually a new temple is built. Under Ezra's leadership, the centrality of God's law as the regulator of all life is reaffirmed.

Soon afterwards, Nehemiah leads a party to rebuild the walls of Jerusalem. Some of the promises have been fulfilled, at least in part, but it is clear that this is not the time of final fulfilment. Those who can remember the good old days before the exile, or have heard tales of them from their grandparents, realize that the new Jerusalem is far less impressive than the old one; but the prophets have foretold something much better. When the foundation for the new temple is laid, some of the younger ones shout for joy. But those who are older and wiser weep (Ezra 3:11–13). They know that this cannot be the new temple Ezekiel prophesied: it is smaller than Solomon's. And the people clearly do not have new hearts: the book of Nehemiah ends in disappointment as he

The kingdom of God	The pattern of the kingdom	The perished kingdom	The promised kingdom	The partial kingdom	The prophesied kingdom
God's people	Adam and Eve	No-one	Abraham's descendants	The Israelites	Remnant of Israel; inclusion of nations
God's place	The garden	Banished	Canaan	Canaan (and Jerusalem and temple)	New temple; new creation
God's rule and blessing	God's word; perfect relationships	Disobedience and curse	Blessing to Israel and the nations	The law and the king	New covenant; new king; great blessing

Figure 27. The prophesied kingdom

laments the fact that God's law is disobeyed, despite Ezra's efforts (Nehemiah 13).

Three prophets, Haggai, Zechariah and Malachi, prophesy at this time (the 'post-exilic prophets'). Their message is much the same as that of their predecessors before the exile. They too have to condemn their hearers for breaking the covenant and warn of coming judgment. But they also point to a time in the future when God will act to fulfil his promises so that his people may enjoy all the blessings of the covenant.

The Hebrew arrangement of the Old Testament closes with 2 Chronicles, which ends with the promise that the exile of God's people will soon be over. In one sense that happens after 538 BC, but that is not the new exodus the prophets spoke of. Spiritually speaking, God's people are still in exile, waiting for the Lord to return to them and fulfil all his promises of salvation. God's kingdom still has not come, because God's king has not come. But the last of the prophets insists that he will appear, preceded by a messenger: 'See, I will send my messenger, who will prepare the way before me. Then suddenly the Lord you are seeking will come to his temple; the messenger of the covenant, whom you desire, will come' (Malachi 3:1).

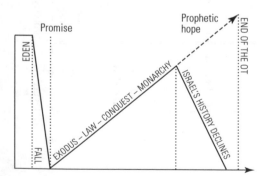

Figure 28. The end of the Old Testament

Bible study

Hosea 1 – 3

What are the different stages in the relationship between Hosea and Gomer, his wife (see chapters 1 and 3)?

How does their marriage mirror the relationship between God and his people?

What do we learn about the people's sin?

How will God judge them?

What hope is there?

What echoes are there, in this hope, of the promises to Abraham and David?

What do we learn about God from this passage?

What do we learn about ourselves from it?

How should our lives change in the light of what we have learned?

6

The present kingdom

The time has come

At first sight we may feel that a genealogy is an uninspiring way to start the New Testament, but, if we remember God's promises, we will be on the edge of our seats as soon as we read the words: 'A record of the genealogy of Jesus Christ the son of David, the son of Abraham' (Matthew 1:1). He is the one who fulfils the promises to Abraham in Genesis 12 and to David in 2 Samuel 7. The apostle Paul expresses it clearly: 'no matter how many promises God has made, they are "yes" in Christ' (2 Corinthians 1:20).

Mark begins his Gospel by quoting from Malachi and Isaiah:

'I will send my messenger ahead of you,
    who will prepare your way' –
'a voice of one calling in the desert,
"Prepare the way for the Lord,
    make straight paths for him."'
(Mark 1:2–3)

Both prophets foretold that a herald would appear in advance of

God's king, to announce his imminent arrival and to urge people to get ready for him. Mark identifies John the Baptist as that herald: 'And so John came, baptising in the desert region and preaching a baptism of repentance for the forgiveness of sins' (1:4). The message is clear: the waiting is over; the exile is about to end and the time of fulfilment is soon to come. And then Jesus appears, 'proclaiming the good news of God. "The time has come," he said. "The kingdom of God is near. Repent and believe the good news!" ' (1:14–15).

'The kingdom of God' is not an expression the Old Testament uses, but Jesus speaks of it often in his teaching. It sums up the prophetic hope. He understands that he has come in fulfilment of all that the Old Testament pointed forward to. He tells his disciples, '. . . blessed are your eyes because they see, and your ears because they hear. For I tell you the truth, many prophets and righteous men longed to see what you see but did not see it, and to hear what you hear but did not hear it' (Matthew 13:16–17). Speaking of the Old Testament, he says, 'These are the Scriptures that testify about me' (John 5:39).

Fulfilment in Christ

The New Testament never leads us to expect that there will be any fulfilment of the Old Testament promises other than their fulfilment in Christ (Figure 29). We are not encouraged, for example, to look for their fulfilment in the State of Israel and to expect a new temple to be built there. That is to expect a renewal of the model that has now been dismantled. The permanent reality is found in Christ. Graeme Goldsworthy has put it like this:

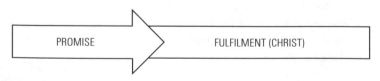

Figure 29. Fulfilment in Christ

'For the New Testament the interpretation of the Old Testament is not "literal" but "Christological". That is to say that the coming of Christ transforms all the kingdom terms of the Old Testament into gospel reality.'[1]

Another writer draws an analogy with a father a century ago, who promises his young son that he will give him a horse on his twenty-first birthday. Cars are subsequently invented, and so, when the birthday finally comes, the boy is given a car instead of a horse. The promise has still been fulfilled, but not literally. The father could not have promised his son a car because neither could have understood the concept. In a similar way, God made his promises to Israel in ways they could understand. He used categories they were familiar with, such as the nation, the temple and material prosperity in the land. But the fulfilment breaks the boundaries of those categories. To expect a literal fulfilment is to miss the point: 'To look for direct fulfilments of, say, Ezekiel in the twentieth-century Middle East, is to bypass and short-circuit the reality and the finality of what we already have in Christ as the fulfilment of those great assurances. It is like taking delivery of the motor car but still expecting to receive a horse.'[2] All the promises of the kingdom of God are fulfilled in Christ; he is God's people, God's place and God's rule.

God's people

Adam, the first man, failed in his role as the image of God and was evicted from the garden. God made a new start with the Israelites, who were called to be his holy people, reflecting his character as they obeyed his law. They too failed and were sent into exile. But, where Adam and Israel failed, Jesus succeeds. He is what the people of God were meant to be: the true Adam and the true Israel.

Jesus is the true Adam

The Gospels stress that Jesus is a real human being. He is born as a baby; he sleeps, weeps, gets tired and even dies. He is descended from Adam (Luke 3:23–38) and identifies with Adam's race in his baptism (Luke 3:21–22). But, unlike Adam, when he is tempted he does not sin. He is the only human being who perfectly obeys God, his Father. He is, therefore, the one person to have lived who does not deserve to be banished from God's presence. But on the cross he willingly faces the punishment that we all deserve, as sinners who are bound up with the first Adam. As a result, if we trust in him, we enter into a new humanity, headed not by Adam, the sinner, but by Jesus, the righteous new Adam. Paul writes, '... just as through the disobedience of one man [Adam] the many were made sinners, so also through the obedience of the one man [Christ] the many will be made righteous' (Romans 5:19; see Figure 30).

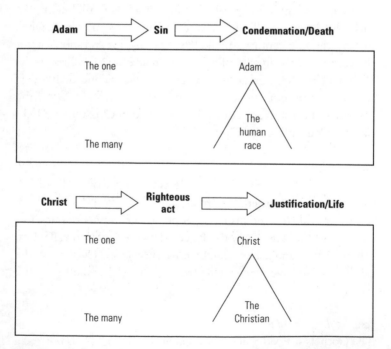

Figure 30. Romans 5:19

Jesus is the true Israel
When Jesus is a child, Joseph and Mary take him to Egypt to protect him from Herod's persecution. Matthew comments: 'So was fulfilled what the Lord had said through the prophet: "Out of Egypt I called my son"' (Matthew 2:15). Some commentators suggest that this is an unprincipled use of Old Testament prophecy. The quotation is from Hosea 11:1, which is not a messianic promise referring to an individual. The original context makes it very clear that it refers to the exodus of the nation of Israel. But Matthew is neither naïve nor unprincipled. He knows exactly what he is doing. He is deliberately identifying Jesus with Israel. But Jesus is different. He too is tempted, as the Israelites were in the wilderness, but, unlike them, he does not fall (Matthew 4:1–11).

He then calls his first disciples. His choice of twelve is no coincidence; it is a deliberate statement. He is calling together a new Israel, with twelve disciples as the foundation, rather than twelve tribes (4:18–22). The old Israel rejects Jesus and will, in turn, be rejected by God. Jesus says, '... the kingdom of God will be taken from you and be given to a people who will produce its fruit' (Matthew 21:43). He foretells the destruction of Jerusalem as the awful expression of that judgment (Luke 19:43–44). It is carried out by the Romans in AD 70. From now on the true Israel is not focused on the land of Palestine and does not consist of those who are physically descended from Abraham. It rather consists of his spiritual descendants: those, both Jew and Gentile, who follow his example and place their trust in God's promise fulfilled in Jesus: '... the promise comes by faith, so that it may be by grace and may be guaranteed to all Abraham's offspring – not only to those who are of the law [i.e. Jews] but also to those who are of the faith of Abraham. He is the father of us all' (Romans 4:16).

God's place
Adam and Eve enjoyed God's presence with them in the garden before the fall. God also drew near to the Israelites, living in their

midst in the tabernacle and then in the temple. But the temple in Jerusalem was just a shadow of what we can receive in Christ. He is the true temple, the place where we may enter perfectly into God's presence. He is not just the true human being; he is also the true God. In Christ, God himself has drawn near to us.

Jesus is the true tabernacle

'The Word became flesh and made his dwelling [or "tabernacled"] among us' (John 1:14).

Jesus is the true temple

After he has cleared the temple of those who had set up their own businesses there, some Jews challenge Jesus to prove his authority to do it. He replies, 'Destroy this temple, and I will raise it again in three days' (John 2:19). They assume he is speaking about the building, but John tells us that 'the temple he had spoken of was his body' (2:21). The temple in Jerusalem is soon to be destroyed. If we want to meet with God we must go, not to a building, but to Jesus (see John 4:21–24). Standing in the temple courts, he says, 'If anyone is thirsty, let him come to me and drink. Whoever believes in me, as the Scripture has said, streams of living water will flow from within him' (John 7:37–38). He is surely thinking of Ezekiel's promise of the new temple, from which a river would flow, bringing life to all (Ezekiel 47). He is that temple, and the water is the Spirit he gives to all who trust in him.

God's rule and blessing

Jesus introduces the new covenant

He has come, not to abolish the law, but to fulfil it (Matthew 5:17). He perfectly obeys its demands, and therefore, uniquely, does not need to face the curse of judgment that must be met by all law-breakers. But on the cross 'Christ redeemed us from the curse of the law by becoming a curse for us'. He dies to take the penalty we deserve so that we may receive the blessings of the covenant through faith in him (Galatians 3:13–14). He lives a perfect life for us and then dies our death for us. As a result, 'the righteous requirements of the law' are 'fully met in us' (Romans 8:4). A wonderful swap takes place. If we have trusted in Christ, we can be sure that he has taken our sin and its judgment, so that he can give us his perfect righteousness: 'God made him who had no sin to be sin for us, so that in him we might become the righteousness of God' (2 Corinthians 5:21). The death of Jesus thus introduces the new covenant: 'Christ is the mediator of a new covenant, that those who are called may receive the promised eternal inheritance – now that he has died as a ransom to set them free from the sins committed under the first covenant' (Hebrews 9:15).

Jesus is the new king

The prophets made it clear that God's promises would be fulfilled by a new king, a descendant of David. He would establish God's rule and introduce a new age in which the evil effects of the fall are undone. The miracles of Jesus point to the fact that he is that king. They are signs of the new creation he has come to establish. When Jesus heals a demon-possessed man, who is also blind and mute, an astonished crowd asks, 'Could this be the son of David?'

The Pharisees reply: 'It is only by Beelzebub [Satan], the prince of demons, that this fellow drives out demons.'

Jesus points out the logical contradiction in their explanation: why would Satan drive out Satan? 'But if I drive out demons by the Spirit of God, then the kingdom of God has come upon you' (Matthew 12:22–28). The kingdom of God has come because God's king has come. At times he does not look much like a king, not least when he dies in weakness on the cross. But that is the moment of his greatest victory, when he defeats his enemies and sets his people free (Colossians 2:13–15). And then, on the third day, he is raised to life again and later ascends to the right hand of the Father. The resurrection proclaims beyond doubt that he is not simply the son of David; he is also the Son of God (Romans 1:4).

Jesus is the source of God's blessing
He says, 'Come to me, all you who are weary and burdened, and I will give you rest' (Matthew 11:28). 'Rest' was the goal of God's creation. That does not mean that we were designed to do nothing, but rather that God wants us to share in his rest, the Sabbath day, which symbolizes the perfection of God's creation. Adam and Eve enjoyed that rest before the fall, as described in Genesis 2; but everything was spoilt by their sin. The Israelites then knew something of it in the promised land in the partial kingdom. But that was just a pale reflection of what God now wants to give us in Christ. By his resurrection he introduces a new age. He faces the penalty of death and comes out the other side. The resurrection marks the beginning of a new age. If we trust in him, we too can pass from death to life. We can experience life as it was designed to be lived by the loving creator: '... if anyone is in Christ, he is a new creation; the old has gone, the new has come' (2 Corinthians 5:17).

The cross: salvation through substitution
There is no hint of embarrassment among the first Christians that their Lord has been killed as a common criminal by a degrading method of execution. Paul even says, 'May I never boast except in the cross of our Lord Jesus Christ, through which the world has been crucified to me, and I to the world' (Galatians 6:14). He knows that the cross is no tragic failure; it is a triumphant success. God's kingdom could have come no other way. Something had to be done about sin and God's anger against it. He could not simply stop being angry; if he did that, he would cease to be God. God's justice demands that he cannot turn a blind eye to evil; it must be punished. God in his grace sent his own Son to take that punishment in our place. He died as a substitute, instead of others, facing God's anger against human sin. He is the one to

The kingdom of God	The pattern of the kingdom	The perished kingdom	The promised kingdom	The partial kingdom	The prophesied kingdom	The present kingdom
God's people	Adam and Eve	No-one	Abraham's descendants	The Israelites	Remnant of Israel; inclusion of nations	*Jesus Christ:* new Adam; new Israel
God's place	The garden	Banished	Canaan	Canaan (and Jerusalem and temple)	New temple; new creation	*Jesus Christ:* true tabernacle; true temple
God's rule and blessing	God's word; perfect relationships	Disobedience and curse	Blessing to Israel and the nations	The law and the king	New covenant; new king; great blessing	*Jesus Christ:* new covenant; rest

Figure 31. The present kingdom

The salvation Christ won for us is so wonderful that no one image can fully express it. The New Testament uses several, all of which result from the fact that Christ died in our place to take our punishment.

Redemption

We have been set free by the payment of a price: '. . . it was not with perishable things such as silver or gold that you were redeemed from the empty way of life handed down to you from your forefathers, but with the precious blood of Christ, a lamb without blemish or fault' (1 Peter 18–19).

Reconciliation

We were God's enemies but now we are his friends: 'All this is from God, who reconciled us to himself through Christ and gave us the ministry of reconciliation' (2 Corinthians 5:18).

Justification

We were under God's condemnation but now we are righteous in his sight: '. . . all have sinned and fall short of the glory of God, and are justified freely by his grace through the redemption that came by Christ Jesus' (Romans 3:23–24).

Conquest

We were powerless in the face of evil spiritual forces who had us in their clutches. But Christ's death releases us from bondage to death and therefore sets us free from Satan's power: 'Having disarmed the principalities and powers, he made a public spectacle of them, triumphing over them by the cross' (Colossians 2:15).

Figure 32. The achievement of the cross

whom the Passover lambs and all the sacrifices of the Old Testament pointed. As a result, God's righteous wrath is satisfied or 'propitiated', and, if we trust in Christ, we need no longer face it. 'Christ died for sins once for all, the righteous for the unrighteous, to bring you to God' (1 Peter 3:18; see also Romans 3:21; 1 John 2:2).

The four Gospels

There are many verbal similarities between the 'synoptic' Gospels (Matthew, Mark and Luke). It seems that there is a literary relationship between the writers, although no-one knows exactly who copied from whom and whether or not any of them relied on another common source. John's Gospel is written in a very different style and contains much material that is unique to him. The Gospels do not contradict one another, but rather give us complementary accounts of what Jesus said and did. Although they have much in common, they each provide their own distinctive contributions to our understanding of Jesus.

Matthew: Jesus is the Christ of the Old Testament Scriptures

Matthew has a primarily Jewish audience in mind and stresses that Jesus came to fulfil the Old Testament. There are over a hundred references to the Old Testament in the Gospel. Twelve times Matthew introduces a quotation by saying something like, 'This took to place to fulfil what the Lord had said through the prophet . . .' (e.g. 1:22; 2:15, 17).

Mark: Jesus is the Suffering Servant who calls us to suffer too

Mark is a gospel in two halves. The first half concludes when Peter recognizes that Jesus is the Christ (8:29). The second half focuses on the cross: 'He then began to teach them that the Son of Man must suffer many things . . . and that he must be killed' (8:31). And his disciples are to walk the path he trod: 'If anyone would come after me, he must deny himself and take up his cross and follow me' (8:34).

Luke: Jesus is the Saviour of the world

Salvation for Luke consists of two great blessings: the forgiveness of sins and the gift of the Holy Spirit. This salvation is not limited to religious people or to Jews; it is for all types and all nations. We see men and women, children and adults, rich and poor, Jews and Gentiles all receiving grace from Jesus. Luke's second volume,

Acts, shows how the good news about him spreads all over the world.

John: Jesus is the Son of God who gives eternal life
John's characteristic description of Jesus is as the eternal, unique Son of God the Father. As such, he makes some staggering claims about himself in the 'I am' sayings, such as 'I am the light of the world' and 'I am the way and the truth and the life' (8:12; 14:6). These claims are supported by a series of miracles, or 'signs'. They are designed to promote faith in Jesus: 'These [signs] are written that you may believe that Jesus is the Christ, the Son of God, and that by believing you may have life in his name' (John 20:31).

The conductor returns

When I go to a classical-music concert, I am always amazed that an orchestra, which consists of so many individuals with very different instruments, can combine to produce such a beautiful sound. They depend on two vital ingredients: a score, which tells them which notes to play, and a conductor, who directs them when they are to play them. It would be disastrous if the orchestra tried to get rid of the conductor: they would not know when to come in or what speed to play at. It would be even worse if they tore up the score.

That is what we humans have done. God is the composer who created this world, and he gave instructions about how we should live; the score he wants us to play. But we ignore them. We would rather play our own notes in our own time, so we dismiss him and tear up his score. It is hardly surprising that there is no harmony in the world. How can there be, if we all insist on playing our own tune? The result is a terrible cacophony. We desperately need a conductor if we are to begin to play the right notes again. There is no hope for the world otherwise.

Jesus is both the composer and the conductor. He has come to restore order. He wants to change the ugly discord of our lives and our world into the beautiful music they were designed to make: a symphony of praise to the Creator. He himself played that perfect music as he lived in perfect submission to God his Father. By his death on the cross he made it possible for us to return to God's orchestra, despite the way we have treated him. Then, by his resurrection, he was established as the eternal conductor. If we take our lead from him we will find our proper place in God's world once more. Our lives will make sense and will begin to produce beautiful music again, bringing praise to God.

But we do not have to be very humble to admit that at the moment we still also produce many discordant notes and we live in a world that is full of discord. The conductor has come, and yet we still disobey him, and many refuse to acknowledge him altogether. To use the language of the Bible, the kingdom of God has come, and yet it has not come in all its fullness. Jesus taught his disciples that he would leave the earth and that there would be a delay before he returned. It is only when he comes again that everything will be put right and all discord will be banished for ever. Our next chapter looks at what the Bible teaches about what we can expect in the meantime, between Jesus' first and second comings.

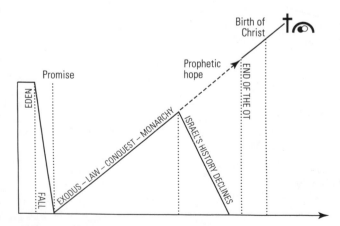

Figure 33. The story so far: the birth of Christ

Bible study

Luke 1:39–80; 2:25–32

What do the words of Mary, Zechariah and Simeon teach us about the salvation Jesus brings?

How do they point to the fulfilment of the following Old Testament passages?

• Genesis 12:1–3

• 2 Samuel 7:11–16

• Isaiah 9:2–7

• Isaiah 42:5–7

• Isaiah 49:5–7

- Jeremiah 31:31–34

- Malachi 3:1

How should we respond?

7

The proclaimed kingdom

We have seen how Jesus fulfils all the promises of God. He is the one to whom the whole Old Testament points: God's king, the Messiah. As soon as the disciples begin to recognize that truth, they expect the kingdom of God to come in all its fullness. The prophets have made it clear that at the time of fulfilment the Messiah will bring about a great division: God's enemies will be judged and his people vindicated. Everything will then be made new for ever. But it has not happened. Instead, Jesus has taught them that he has to die. Far from defeating God's enemies, he is defeated by them; at least, that is how it looks.

It is not surprising that the disciples are discouraged when Jesus dies. They still have not understood from the prophets that the Christ has to die if God's kingdom is to come. Hope returns on the first Easter day when Jesus rises again. He has been vindicated: he really is the Messiah, as he has claimed. But still the great division has not come. The disciples should not be surprised. Jesus has often told them how he would leave the earth and return only after a delay (e.g. Matthew 24:36 – 25:46). The promises of the kingdom will not be completely fulfilled until his second coming.

Jesus tells us to be ready for that day: 'Keep watch, because you do not know the day or the hour' (Matthew 25:13).

The last days

The Bible calls the time between the first and second comings of Christ 'the last days' (e.g. 2 Timothy 3:1; James 5:3). This is the period in which the New Testament letters were written and in which we still live today. It lies in the intersection of two ages: 'this present age' and 'the age to come' (e.g. Matthew 12:32; see Figure 34). The kingdom of God is both 'now' and 'not yet'. It has come with the appearance of Jesus on earth and through his death and resurrection. He has spoken of the kingdom as a present reality. It has been manifest in his own ministry on earth and it is now possible for anyone to enter it (e.g. Matthew 12:28; 19:14; etc.). But the kingdom is also something we must wait for in the future. It is only when Jesus returns that it will be fully introduced and Jesus will say to his people, 'Come, you who are blessed by my Father; take your inheritance, the kingdom prepared for you since the creation of the world' (Matthew 25:34). If we have placed our trust in Christ, we belong to the new creation, but we have not yet received all its blessings. For the time being we must live in a fallen world, which bears the marks of sin and of God's judgment against it.

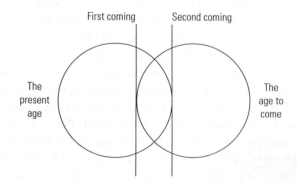

Figure 34. The kingdom, now and not yet

The reason for the delay

Peter predicts that sceptics will wonder whether Jesus will ever return: '. . . in the last days scoffers will come, scoffing and following their own evil desires. They will say, "Where is this 'coming' he promised?"' (2 Peter 3:3–4). He encourages Christians: '. . . do not forget this one thing, dear friends: With the Lord a day is like a thousand years and a thousand years are like a day. The Lord is not slow in keeping his promise, as some understand slowness. He is patient with you, not wanting anyone to perish, but everyone to come to repentance' (verses 8–9). Two thousand years is not long from God's perspective. He has deliberately delayed the return of the Lord Jesus so that more people have a chance to hear the gospel and repent before it is too late. That is why I have called this period 'the proclaimed kingdom'. It is the age of gospel proclamation to all nations, as Jesus himself made clear.

Just before Jesus ascended to heaven, he tells his disciples, 'This is what is written: The Christ will suffer and rise from the dead on the third day, and repentance and forgiveness of sins will be preached in his name to all nations, beginning at Jerusalem. You are witnesses of these things. I am going to send you what my Father has promised; but stay in the city until you have been clothed with power from on high' (Luke 24:46–49). There is a command and a promise. The command is to proclaim the gospel in all the world. That is a massive task for a small group of weak and frightened individuals. But they are not left on their own. God promises to give them power: the presence of the Holy Spirit in their lives.

The same command and promise are found at the beginning of Acts, Luke's second volume. It continues the story from the ascension of Jesus to the early years of the Christian church. The disciples ask Jesus, 'Lord, are you at this time going to restore the kingdom to Israel?' (1:6). Their question reveals how little they understand of what Jesus has taught them. They still have not grasped that Jesus' concern is not limited to Israel; it is for all people everywhere. And they still do not realize that there must be a delay before he returns, a period in which the gospel is proclaimed throughout the world in the power of the Spirit.

Jesus replies, 'It is not for you to know times or dates the Father has set by his own authority. But you will receive power when the Holy Spirit comes on you; and you will be my witnesses in Jerusalem, and in all Judea and Samaria, and to the ends of the earth' (1:7–8).

Having said those words, Jesus ascends into heaven. An angel then reassures them, 'This same Jesus, who has been taken from you into heaven, will come back in the same way you have seen him go into heaven' (1:11). But first they have a job to do. Jesus had said, '. . . this gospel of the kingdom will be preached in the whole world as a testimony to the nations, and then the end will come' (Matthew 24:14).

The sending of the Spirit

The first Christians do not have long to wait before they receive the gift of the Spirit. They are gathered together in one place on the day of Pentecost when the Holy Spirit comes upon them. Immediately they begin to preach the gospel in other 'tongues' (or 'languages'). That is a very clear sign that the Spirit has been given for a specific purpose: to help them spread the good news about Christ throughout the world. God is at work reversing the effects of the confusion of languages, which was his judgment after the building of the tower of Babel (Genesis 11). In the past the nations were divided, but now, through the gospel, God is calling together a multinational family of people, united in the Lord Jesus Christ. The bystanders do not understand that at the time. They cannot work out what is happening. Peter explains that God

1. The sending of the Spirit	2. The gospel preached to all nations	3. Jesus returns

Figure 35. A chronology of the last days

is fulfilling his promise through the prophet Joel: 'In the last days, God says, I will pour out my Spirit on all people' (Acts 2:17).

We might call the last days 'the age of the Spirit'. Of course, he had been active before: the Spirit is the eternal God. But in Old Testament times he had lived only within certain special individuals, such as kings and prophets, to equip them for particular tasks. But now he will fill all of God's people. All of them will receive power to prophesy in his name, telling others about the Lord Jesus. The rest of the book of Acts tells the story of how that begins to happen, as the gospel gradually spreads from Jerusalem to Judea, Samaria and the ends of the earth in fulfilment of the words of Jesus in 1:8. It concludes with Paul in Rome, the centre of the known world.

Two thousand years later, God continues to be patient and is still delaying his judgment. It is our responsibility to tell the good news of Christ in the power of the Spirit to as many people as possible.

The work of the Spirit

It is by his Spirit that God is at work extending his kingdom in these last days. His work includes the following great ministries.

He brings new birth

Jesus told Nicodemus that 'no-one can see the kingdom of God unless he is born again' (John 3:3). We are all by nature rebels against God, and would never of ourselves repent and put our trust in Christ; it needs a miracle if that is to happen. The great work of God the Holy Spirit is to perform that miracle. Jesus taught that to be born again we need to be 'born of the Spirit' (John 3:5). The Spirit convicts us of our sin (John 16:7–11), and then points us to Jesus as the one who can deal with it. His concern is to focus attention, not on himself, but on Jesus, who said of him, 'He will bring glory to me by taking from what is mine and making it known to you' (John 16:14). As he points us to Jesus, he opens our eyes to understand the truth about him

As the creator of everyone, God has always had a concern for all nations, not just Israel.

- *The promised kingdom*. God promised Abraham, ' . . . all peoples on earth will be blessed through you' (Genesis 12:3). He will be a 'father of many nations' (17:5).

- *The partial kingdom*. Israel was meant to be a 'kingdom of priests' (Exodus 19), acting as a mediator between God and the nations. Some foreigners share in God's blessing to them: for example, Rahab (Joshua 6), the Queen of Sheba (1 Kings 10) and Naaman (2 Kings 5).

- *The prophesied kingdom*. God's servant will be 'a light for the Gentiles' and 'all the ends of the earth will see the salvation of our God' (Isaiah 42:6; 52:10).

- *The present kingdom*. Jesus' earthly ministry was focused on the Jews (Matthew 15:24), but he did bring salvation to Gentiles too (e.g. Matthew 8:5–13; 15:21–28). He taught that Israel's rejection of him would lead to God's judgment on her. Then the gospel would be proclaimed to all nations (Matthew 21:43; 24:14).

- *The proclaimed kingdom*. Christian believers have been given the Spirit to equip us to take the gospel to all people. Mission is not an option for the keen few; it is an obligation for us all. Jesus commands us to 'go and make disciples of all nations' (Matthew 28:19).

- *The perfected kingdom*. God's family in heaven will include representatives 'from every nation, tribe, people and language' (Revelation 7:9).

Figure 36. God and the nations

(1 Thessalonians 1:4–5) and enables us to put our trust in him. At that moment we are born again and he comes into our lives. All believers have the Spirit living within them; we could not be Christians otherwise: ' . . . if anyone does not have the Spirit of Christ, he does not belong to Christ' (Romans 8:9).

This miracle of new birth is produced by the Spirit through God's word. We must never divide the word and the Spirit as if they operate in different spheres. Paul tells us that the word of God is the 'sword of the Spirit' (Ephesians 6:17). Peter reminds his readers that 'you have been born again, not of perishable seed, but of imperishable, through the living and enduring word of God' (1 Peter 1:23). He is not contradicting Jesus' teaching that we are born again by the Spirit. It is as the word of God (the gospel found in the Bible) is proclaimed that the Spirit works to call people to Christ.

He equips us to serve Christ
We have seen already that the Spirit was given to enable us to fulfil the Great Commission of Jesus to take the gospel to all nations. On our own we are weak and frightened, but with the Spirit's help we can have the courage to stand up for Christ in a hostile world.

Soon after the day of Pentecost, Peter and John are imprisoned for preaching the gospel and then summoned before the Sanhedrin, the Jewish ruling council. They must be frightened; their lives are in danger. Only weeks before, they watched Jesus being crucified, and they know that they could face the same fate. It must be tempting to compromise, but, instead, Peter boldly speaks of Christ. Luke explains the secret of his courage: he is 'filled with the Holy Spirit' (Acts 4:8). We should pray that the same Spirit will give us the strength to be bold in our witness for Christ today. We cannot claim to be filled with the Spirit as individuals or as churches if we are not active in evangelism; the Spirit's great concern is to lead people to Christ.

The Spirit also equips us in our ministry to one another. Each of us has received spiritual gifts that God wants us to use for the benefit of other Christians. We are members of one body, designed by God to work together for the glory of his name (1 Corinthians 12:12–31). Just as each part of the body has an important contribution to make, so each individual Christian has been gifted by God for the sake of the whole body: 'to each one the manifestation of the Spirit is given for the common good' (1 Corinthians 12:7).

He produces holiness
The Bible uses three tenses to speak of our salvation (Figure 37). If we trust in Christ, we have already been saved, in the past, from the *penalty* of sin by the death of Christ: 'By grace you have been saved' (Ephesians 2:8). We shall have nothing to fear on judgment day because Christ has already faced our punishment in our place. But sin, sadly, is very much a reality in our lives. It is only in the future, after Christ returns, that we shall be saved from the *presence* of sin. So the Bible sometimes speaks of our salvation as something that is still to come. We shall receive its full blessings only in the future (e.g. 1 Corinthians 3:15; 1 Timothy 2:15). That just leaves the present tense (e.g. 1 Corinthians 1:18; 15:2). We are being saved, in the present, from the *power* of sin. Although we shall never be sinless this side of heaven, God is at work within us by his Spirit to help us fight sin in our lives and become more like Jesus. We must certainly play our part and work hard to resist evil, but we are not left to do so on our own. It is 'by the Spirit' that we are to 'put to death the misdeeds of the body' (Romans 8:13).

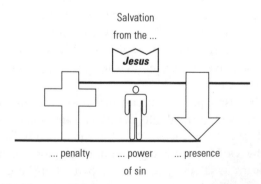

Figure 37. The three tenses of salvation

The kingdom of God

During the last days, the kingdom of God is spreading as the Spirit works through the proclamation of the gospel. The promises of the kingdom are being fulfilled in remarkable ways.

God's people

The new Israel is the church, all those who trust in Christ. Peter writes to a Christian audience, consisting primarily of Gentiles, and boldly applies to them some of the titles that had previously been the property of the Israelites alone: 'You are a chosen people, a royal priesthood, a holy nation, a people belonging to God' (1 Peter 2:9). Paul insists in his letters that Gentiles do not have to be circumcised, or obey the ritual requirements of the Jewish law (such as kosher food regulations), to be full members of God's family. We are justified by faith alone and not by anything we do. The true Israelite, or member of the people of God, is not simply someone who is physically descended from Abraham and outwardly obeys the Jewish law, but rather the converted believer in Christ: 'A man is not a Jew if he is only one outwardly, nor is circumcision merely outward and physical. No, a man is a Jew if he is one inwardly; and circumcision is circumcision of the heart, by the Spirit, not by the written code' (Romans 2:28–29).

God's place

The Lord Jesus, the true temple of God, has now ascended to heaven, but God continues to live in this fallen world. His temple now is not a holy building but a holy people. Paul reminds us that the Holy Spirit lives within each of us individually: ' . . . your body is a temple of the Holy Spirit, who is in you, whom you have received from God'. The application is obvious: 'honour God with your body' (1 Corinthians 6:19–20). God also lives within us as a Christian community. Paul describes the church as a building 'built on the foundation of the apostles and prophets, with Christ Jesus himself as the chief cornerstone. In him the whole building is joined together and rises to become a holy temple in the Lord' (Ephesians 2:20–21; see also 1 Peter 2:4–5).

God's rule and blessing

God's law reflects his eternal character and is 'holy, righteous and good' (Romans 7:12). But our sin meant that it became a harsh taskmaster that held us in bondage. We were powerless to obey it and, therefore, powerless to escape its condemnation: 'no-one will be declared righteous in [God's] sight by observing the law; rather, through the law we become conscious of sin' (Romans 3:20). But Christ has now set us free from this bondage to sin, the law and death (which is the penalty for law-breaking) by facing the penalty in our place. We can therefore enjoy the blessings of the new covenant. We have the presence of the Spirit within us to help us live up to God's standards: 'now, by dying to what once bound us, we have been released from the law so that we serve in the new way of the Spirit, and not in the old way of the written code' (Romans 7:6).

Christian experience in the last days

We have so much to thank God for as Christians. He has given us the wonderful gifts of forgiveness for all our sins, adoption into his family, fellowship with the Holy Spirit and the certain hope of heaven. We should be full of joy. Peter writes: 'Though you have not seen [Christ], you love him; and even though you do not see him now, you believe in him and are filled with an inexpressible and glorious joy, for you are receiving the goal of your faith, the salvation of your souls' (1 Peter 1:8–9). But it is not all joy for the Christian in these last days. We shall also have to 'suffer grief in all kinds of trials' (1 Peter 1:6). We are not in heaven yet.

The Christian's experience is one of frustration as well as joy. Paul writes that 'we ourselves, who have the firstfruits of the Spirit, groan inwardly as we wait eagerly for our adoption as sons, the redemption of our bodies' (Romans 8:23). We have received so much, 'the firstfruits of the Spirit'. We still live in a fallen world, and yet God has given us the Spirit, who belongs to the age to come. We have a taste of heaven on earth; we can know something of its blessings already. But our salvation is far from complete. For example, our bodies are still not redeemed. Christians will decay and die along with everyone else. Our faith in Christ does not grant us immunity from wrinkles, grey hairs, broken legs or cancer. And the world we live in is still not redeemed. We shall continue to struggle against sin and to face opposition for our faith. The Christian life is hard work; it is a fight and a race (2 Timothy 4:7). Do not be surprised if you find it a struggle to live for Christ; that is the normal Christian life in this present world. The presence of the Spirit certainly helps, but it also contributes to the sense of frustration we feel.

Have you ever been in the kitchen when someone is baking some delicious food? The cook lets you have a taste before giving you strict instructions not to touch any more until it is served on the table later. The anticipation is almost unbearable. It would have been easier if you had not been allowed that taste. But now that you know how delicious it is, you find it very hard to wait for another mouthful. Those two hours before the meal seem like an eternity.

It is similar for us in the Christian life. We have the firstfruits of the Spirit: a taste of the blessings of heaven. We know something of what it is like to be holy, and we long for more. And we know something of what it means to know God through Christ and to be loved by him, and we cannot wait to feel it more. That is why we 'groan inwardly'. It expresses our frustration with the sin that is so prevalent in our lives and in the world, and signals our desire for more of the wonders of the world to come. That sense of frustration will never leave us in this age. It is an inevitable consequence of the fact that we live in this 'in-between period', in the intersection of the ages. We must not expect life to be easy. We are called to proclaim the gospel to a world that does not want to hear it and to live a Christian life among people who live in a very different way. We are citizens of heaven, who must, for

The kingdom of God	The pattern of the kingdom	The perished kingdom	The promised kingdom	The partial kingdom	The prophesied kingdom	The present kingdom	The proclaimed kingdom
God's people	Adam and Eve	No-one	Abraham's descendants	The Israelites	Remnant of Israel; inclusion of nations	*Jesus Christ:* new Adam; new Israel	The new Israel: Jew and Gentile believers in Christ
God's place	The garden	Banished	Canaan	Canaan (and Jerusalem and temple)	New temple; new creation	*Jesus Christ:* true tabernacle; true temple	The individual believer; the church
God's rule and blessing	God's word; perfect relation-ships	Disobedi-ence and curse	Blessing to Israel and the nations	The law and the king	New covenant; new king; great blessing	*Jesus Christ:* new covenant; rest	New covenant; Holy Spirit

Figure 38. The proclaimed kingdom

the time being, live as 'strangers' in the world (Philippians 3:20; 1 Peter 1:1). But we shall not have to live away from home for ever. One day the Lord Jesus will return to take us to join him in the perfected kingdom.

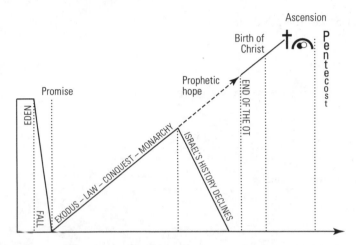

Figure 39. The story so far: Pentecost

 **Bible study**

2 Corinthians 4

Paul has spoken in 2 Corinthians 3 about the new-covenant ministry God has given him. This is the proclamation of the gospel, which leads to righteousness and life, as opposed to the law, which brings condemnation and death. All Christians have the privilege of being involved in this wonderful ministry, the work of evangelism.

4:1–6
What can we learn from Paul's example in evangelism?

What makes the job difficult?

What encouragements are we given?

4:7–12
What is 'this treasure'?

In what sense are we 'jars of clay'?

How do verses 8–9 reflect your experience in evangelism?

Why has God allowed us to be weak?

What encouragements are we given in our weakness?

4:13–18
What is our hope?

What difference should that make to us now?

Summary
How has God challenged you through this passage?

What can you do to try to put its message into practice?

8

The perfected kingdom

We have been waiting for 2,000 years for Jesus' return, but the delay will not go on for ever. This world is heading for a conclusion. Just as God fulfilled his promises in the first coming of Jesus, so he will fulfil his promises about his second coming. Jesus will come again and complete God's eternal plan of salvation; he will introduce the perfected kingdom.

The book of Revelation

Revelation is the last book of the Bible. It was probably written by the apostle John while he was exiled on the island of Patmos. We cannot be sure when he wrote, but the content of the book suggests a time of extreme persecution. The most likely date is during the time of the Emperor Domitian (AD 81–96). It is written in a style of literature known as 'apocalpytic', which uses symbolism to convey its message (other examples in the Bible are found in Daniel 7 – 12 and Zechariah 1 – 6). 'Apocalypse' means 'revelation' or 'unveiling'. God gives John a series of visions in which he pulls back the curtain to reveal what is going on behind the scenes of human history. These visions are designed to

1:1–20	Introduction
2:1 – 3:20	Letters to the seven churches
4:1 – 5:14	A vision of heaven
6:1 – 8:5	The seven seals of destiny
8:6 – 11:19	The seven trumpets of warning
12:1 – 15:4	Conflict between the church and the power of evil
15:5 – 16:21	The seven bowls of punishment
17:1 – 20:15	The triumph of God and the fall of Babylon
21:1 – 22:5	The new heaven and new earth
22:6–21	Epilogue

Figure 40. An outline of Revelation

strengthen believers to persevere, despite their suffering. We are invited to lift up our eyes from the struggles of living for Christ in this present world and look instead at his kingdom, both present and future.

A throne in heaven

The book begins with letters from the Lord Jesus to seven churches in Asia Minor, urging them to stay faithful. Then John is shown a vision: 'At once I was in the Spirit, and there before me was a throne in heaven with someone sitting on it' (4:2). That vision must come as a great relief to the suffering Christians of the first century. There is very little sign of the kingdom of God on earth during their persecution. But, whatever it may feel like, God is in control. There is a throne in heaven and it is not empty.

Imagine you are walking on the coast looking out to sea. You notice a girl swimming not far from the shore and then, to your horror, you see a shark approaching her. You shout for help but no-one listens. The others around you all see what is happening but seem completely unconcerned. You run round the corner to try to get some help, and there you see a big, black chair with one word written on the back of it in capitals: DIRECTOR. A man sits on it with a big cigar and a loud voice, shouting instructions through a megaphone. You heave a sigh of relief: you have stumbled on to a film set. The director has everything under control.

That is the effect of the vision in Revelation 4. Whatever the appearances, God is in control. He is the great director of the universe, sitting on a throne. And we soon discover that the Lord Jesus is there as well. John writes: 'Then I saw a Lamb, looking as if it had been slain, standing in the centre of the throne' (5:6). Jesus is the divine king of the universe. He has suffered and has triumphed; and his death guarantees that all those who suffer for him on earth will also triumph. We may not understand what he is doing in the world, but we can be absolutely sure that he is in charge. God is king. The elders in John's vision respond to that truth in the only appropriate way: they lay their crowns before the throne and worship:

'To him who sits upon the throne and to the Lamb
be praise and honour and glory and power,
            for ever and ever.'
(5:13)

If we are wise we shall follow their example and worship God here on earth. There will be times when that is inconvenient and might cause us hardship, but it is worth it. Whatever the appearances, God alone is in charge. He is the king, even if many do not yet recognize his kingdom.

Interpreting Revelation

The next few chapters of Revelation are dominated by sequences of divine judgments: seven seals, seven trumpets and seven bowls. Included within them are some of the famous characters of the book, such as the four horsemen of the apocalypse and the beast. Over the years, there have been many attempts to interpret who, or what, they represent. Some have argued that all the symbols refer exclusively to people or institutions at the time John was writing (the 'preterist' view). Others see the book as presenting a chronological account of the different eras through history from the first century to the second coming (the 'historicist' view). Still others think that, from chapter 4 onwards, Revelation describes only the events at the very end of the world, in the short period leading up to the return of Christ (the 'futurist' view).

Each of those positions has problems. It is better to see the book as describing what will happen in the whole of 'the last days' between the ascension of Christ and his second coming. Revelation is not written to give us a time chart. We have in the book a number of sequences arranged in parallel. The seals, the trumpets and the bowls do not follow on from one another; they all describe the same period. So, for example, the four horsemen have been active, and will be active, throughout the last days. They represent the imperialistic aggression, bloodshed, economic instability and death that will mark every age until Christ returns. Christians will have to hold firmly to the vision of the throne in heaven if they are to persevere through such hardships. And we shall need to remind ourselves that they will not go on for ever. The last few chapters of the book take us to the end of time when Jesus will destroy evil and establish the perfect new creation.

Out with the old

There is a popular programme on television in which a team visits a house to give it a makeover. We watch as a room is transformed before our eyes. The first part of the procedure is always destructive. That brown and yellow wallpaper was so fashionable when it was put up thirty years ago, but it cannot stay now. The lime-green vinyl flooring has to be pulled up and put on the skip, along with the shabby hardboard that had been fixed to the wall to cover a beautiful Victorian fireplace. It has all got to go. The new materials can be introduced only when the rubbish has gone. 'Out with the old', and only then 'in with the new'. If that is true of a single room, it is also true of the whole world. God cannot introduce the new creation he has promised until all that spoils the old one has been removed.

Down the ages, many have longed for a brave new world. The Marxists thought that all would be well if they could only abolish capitalism and greed. The secular humanists thought the key was the elimination of ignorance and poverty. Revolutionaries have placed their hope in the downfall of a government. But they have all failed to produce lasting change; Utopia remains elusive. That is because they have not dealt with the root of the problem. Ultimately, it is not capitalism, ignorance or wicked government that spoils life on earth; it is, rather, the power of evil, originating from Satan himself. Revelation 17 – 20 uses picture language to describe how God will destroy this power at the end of time, and thus make it possible for him to create a new world, completely free from evil.

The fall of Babylon

In Revelation 17 we are introduced to a woman identified as 'BABYLON THE GREAT / THE MOTHER OF PROSTITUTES / AND OF THE ABOMINATIONS OF THE EARTH' (verse 5). Babylon has already featured significantly in the Bible. It was the location of the Tower of Babel, a symbol of human arrogance and pride (Genesis 11). And it was the capital city of the mighty empire that overtook the kingdom of Judah, destroyed the temple in Jerusalem and took its people into exile. Given that history, it is quite natural for John to give the name 'Babylon' to this woman. She represents non-Christian society organized without reference to God: 'the world'. She is called a 'prostitute' because 'With her the kings of the earth committed adultery and the inhabitants of the earth were intoxicated with the wine of her adulteries' (verse 2). The adultery is spiritual rather than sexual: she seduces many to live for her, rather than for the one true God. But Christians must resist her advances. Like the people of Judah in the sixth century BC, we are in exile. We belong to heaven, but we must live in a foreign land: Babylon, the world. It will often be hostile to us and it will be tempting to compromise and go along with the prevailing spirit. But we must resist the temptation to go to bed with the prostitute, because she is heading for destruction.

The fall of Babylon is described in Revelation 18. An angel proclaims in a loud voice, 'Fallen! Fallen is Babylon the great!' (verse 2). Then another angel hurls a large stone into the sea and says,

'With such violence
    the great city of Babylon will be thrown down,
    never to be found again.'
(verse 21)

It is a comprehensive and final judgment. The proud city of human society, established in stubborn independence from God, will collapse in an instant. All those who have invested everything in her will weep and mourn:

'Woe! Woe, O great city,
    O Babylon, city of power!
In one hour your doom has come!'
(verse 10)

'The beast' (who represents worldly anti-Christian powers), 'the false prophet' (worldly anti-Christian ideology) and Satan are also judged alongside Babylon. They are thrown into the lake of burning sulphur, where they can do no more harm (20:10). And human beings must stand before God in judgment as well. All those whose names are not in the book of life are thrown into the lake of fire, which represents eternal death, separation from God (20:15). All those who refuse to acknowledge Christ's rule must be excluded; God is determined that nothing will be allowed to destroy his perfected kingdom. Judgment is terrible, but it is also good news. Justice is done and evil is destroyed. God's final work of salvation can now be completed.

Many books have been written on the question of the millennium, and churches have split over the issue. The debate concerns the chronology of the events described in Revelation 20:1–10. John watches an angel seize Satan and bind him for a thousand years. This period is not meant to be understood literally; it stands for a long time. During the same thousand-year period, dead Christians are raised to life and reign with Christ. Then, at the end of the millennium, Satan is released from captivity and gathers the powers of the world for a final great battle against God, after which he is finally destroyed.

When is this thousand-year period? Opinions differ.

Postmillennialism
The millennium is the time immediately before the second coming: he will return after it ('post'). This 'millennial age' will be a period of peace and righteousness in which more and more people will become Christians and the world will grow more godly.

Premillennialism
Christ will return before ('pre') the millennium. He will raise dead Christians to life again and they will reign with him on earth. Satan will have no power until the very end of this period, when he will gather together all those who still resist Christ's rule. They will then be destroyed in a final battle, and the end will come.

Amillennialism
The millennium represents the whole of the last days; we are in it now. This is my view.[1] Satan has already been defeated and bound by the death and resurrection of Christ. He is still active, but he can do nothing to thwart God's purposes. Christians who have died already reign with Christ in heaven.

Figure 41. The millennium

In with the new

We have seen how God will destroy Babylon at the end of time. That judgment has a constructive purpose. Once God has thrown this present world on to the scrap heap, he is able to create the new world he promised through the prophets. The last two chapters of Revelation use a variety of images from the Old Testament to describe that new world. It is the new creation, the new Jerusalem and the new temple.

The new creation

> I saw a new heaven and a new earth, for the first heaven and the first earth had passed away.
> (21:1)

God is establishing a completely new creation: a new earth and a new universe ('heaven' here simply refers to the skies). He created everything and he is concerned for all that he has made. The fall affected the whole created order, and salvation, if it is to be complete, must do so as well. God is determined to renew not just our souls but our bodies too, and the environment in which we live. We shall be physical people in a physical place (see 1 Corinthians 15:35–49). That explains why Paul speaks of the whole created order waiting 'in eager expectation' for the end of time. Then at last it will 'liberated from its bondage to decay' (Romans 8:19–21). The frustrating cycle of life followed by death, which is built into the present world, will be broken. There will be no death or decay in the new creation, and no earthquakes or volcano eruptions. In fact, there will be none of the things that currently spoil life on earth: 'There will be no more death or mourning or crying or pain, for the old order of things has passed away' (Revelation 21:4).

The Bible begins with a picture of the world as it was designed by its loving creator. Human beings, Adam and Eve, are in a physical place, the garden of Eden, enjoying perfect harmony with the rest of the created order. That harmony is destroyed by the fall, but God will restore it. Isaiah prophesies that one day an infant will play happily by the hole of the cobra and put its hand into the viper's nest; the wolf and the lion will feed together (11:8; 65:25). Those great promises will be fulfilled. Eden will be restored. Revelation 22 paints a picture of the new creation that deliberately uses some of the landmarks familiar from Genesis 2. As in Eden, there will be a river flowing through the garden with the tree of life beside it (verses 1–3).

An elderly lady hobbled into church recently and said to me, 'You don't happen to know where I can find some new legs, do you?'

I replied, 'Not in this world; but you'll get them in the next. Do you mind waiting for a while?'

She said, 'No, that's worth waiting for.'

She is right. The new creation is not here yet, but it is certainly worth waiting for.

The new Jerusalem

> I saw the Holy City, the new Jerusalem, coming down out of heaven from God.
>
> (21:2)

This is not a new vision; it explains the vision of the new creation that John has just seen: the new creation is a city. The tower of Babel (Babylon) is a symbol of human attempts to create a perfect world by our own efforts. It begins on earth and tries to reach up to the heavens, but it is doomed to failure. By contrast, God's city, the new Jerusalem has a label on it that says, 'Made in heaven'. It comes down from him. He alone is its creator.

Perhaps it is a surprise to find that heaven is described as a city. Many people imagine perfection as an idyllic spot in the country-side, miles away from anyone else. But God's great goal for us is that we shall no longer be isolated from one another, but shall rather be a perfect community, united in Christ. Believers from all ages and countries will be there: 144,000 in number. That figure stands for the totality of God's people; none will be missing. John tells us they are 'a great multitude that no-one could count'. That should warn us not to take the number of 144,000 literally; even a child can count that far, with sufficient patience. There are representatives 'from every nation, tribe, people and language' (7:4–9). God judged humanity after the tower of Babel and scattered us into different nations and languages, but one day that curse will be undone. God's new community will be a multiracial, multicultural society uniting black and white, male and female, Serb and Croat, Arab and Jew. The church on earth should already be reflecting that glorious vision.

The new temple

> I heard a loud voice from the throne saying, 'Now the
> dwelling of God is with men, and he will live with them.
> They will be his people, and God himself will be their God.'
> (21:3)

In the old days God had lived with his people in the temple in Jerusalem. After the destruction of the temple by the Babylonians, God had prophesied through Ezekiel that he would build a new temple. That promise has already been fulfilled through the life, death and resurrection of Jesus. As Christian believers, we know his presence with us by his Holy Spirit; the church is God's temple on earth. But, although we do know God by the Spirit, that knowledge is limited in our experience, and we long to know him more. One day we shall.

It is striking that the city John sees is a perfect cube, just like the Holy of Holies in the temple, where God's presence had been focused. The Holy of Holies was a small area, and only one man, the high priest, was able to enter it, which he did once a year. But now the whole city is the Holy of Holies. It is a cube of 12,000

The kingdom of God	The pattern of the kingdom	The perished kingdom	The promised kingdom	The partial kingdom	The prophesied kingdom	The present kingdom	The proclaimed kingdom	The perfected kingdom
God's people	Adam and Eve	No-one	Abraham's descendants	The Israelites	Remnant of Israel; inclusion of nations	Jesus Christ: new Adam; new Israel	The new Israel: Jew and Gentile believers in Christ	Multi-national family of God
God's place	The garden	Banished	Canaan	Canaan (and Jerusalem and temple)	New temple; new creation	Jesus Christ: true tabernacle; true temple	The individual believer; the church	New creation, new Jerusalem, new temple
God's rule and blessing	God's word; perfect relationships	Disobedience and curse	Blessing to Israel and the nations	The law and the king	New covenant; new king; great blessing	Jesus Christ: new covenant; rest	New covenant; Holy Spirit	Throne of God and the Lamb; perfect blessing

Figure 42. The perfected kingdom

stadia (21:16). That is 1,500 miles square, an area as large as the known world in John's day. The point is clear: there will be no special place in the new creation where God's presence will be concentrated and no holy building to go to if we want to meet with him. The whole place is a temple. That is why we read, 'I did not see a temple in the city, because the Lord God Almighty and the Lamb are its temple' (21:22). There will be no distance between us and God any more; we shall know him perfectly.

The kingdom of God

The promises of the kingdom will all be completely fulfilled at the end of time. God's people will consist of all those, from every nation, who trust in Christ. They will be united together in God's place, the new creation and new Jerusalem, which is the new temple. And they will all submit to God's rule and therefore know his perfect blessing. The throne of God and of the Lamb is right at the centre of everything, and from it a river flows, bringing life and prosperity to everyone (22:1–2).

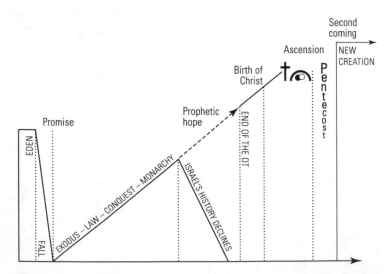

Figure 43. The story so far: new creation

But all this is still to come. The New Testament ends where the Old Testament ended: looking forward; waiting for the final fulfilment of the promises of God. Jesus reassures his people, 'Yes, I am coming soon.' And, if we understand the wonder of what is in store for us, we reply, 'Amen. Come, Lord Jesus' (22:20).

 **Bible study**

Revelation 21:1–8; 21:22 – 22:5

21:1–8
What images are used to describe the perfected kingdom?

How do they build on previous passages in the Bible?

What are the features of life in the new creation?

Who will enjoy its benefits?

• What does it mean to be 'thirsty'?

- What does it mean to 'overcome'?

21:22 – 22:5
How is the perfected kingdom described?

How does the description build on other passages of the Bible?

How does it reflect the garden of Eden?

Who will enjoy this new creation?

What should be the implication of these truths about the future for our lives now?

Epilogue

When Jesus walked with some disciples on the road to Emmaus, he 'explained to them what was said in all the Scriptures concerning himself' (Luke 24:27). I have tried to imagine what he might have told them in that Bible study. My goal in this book has been to show how the whole Bible points to the Lord Jesus. And my prayer is that as a result we may experience three things:

- *Knowing Christ in all the Scriptures.* I hope that sections of the Bible that were previously closed to you have now been opened up and that you can begin to see how they contribute to the overall subject of Jesus Christ and God's plan to establish his kingdom through him.
- *Teaching Christ from all the Scriptures.* Perhaps you have the privilege of teaching others in a Bible-study group, Sunday-school class or church. Now that you have seen the big picture of the Bible, you should be equipped to point people to Christ from any part of it, rather than from just a few favourite passages.
- *Loving Christ through all the Scriptures.* It would be a terrible thing if a deeper knowledge of the Bible affected only our

heads and not our hearts. The Bible is a relational book, which the Holy Spirit uses to help us grow in the knowledge and love of God through Jesus Christ.

The two dimensions

Try to remember two dimensions when you read any passage in the Bible: the historical and the relational. (See Figures 44 and 45.) Ask yourself: 'Where are we in the Bible's storyline? Where have we come from and where are we heading? Which chapter are we in: partial, prophesied, present or proclaimed?' If you are looking at a passage in the Old Testament you will need to consider, 'How is this fulfilled in Christ?' We cannot look at King David in 2 Samuel, for instance, without considering how his kingship points to the perfect king, Jesus. And if you are in the New Testament you may need to ask, 'How does this fulfil what has gone before?'

Figure 44. The historical dimension: promise and fulfilment

This book has been written to help you answer those questions. I hope it makes you feel that you now have a map in your head that gives you the big picture. The result should be that, wherever you land in the Bible, you can find your way around and know where you are in the overall story of God's unfolding plan to save the world through Christ.

But that historical dimension is not the only dimension we should consider when we read the Bible.

In our desire to take seriously the horizontal, chronological element in the Bible, we must not forget the vertical (see Figure 45). For example, the message of an Old Testament passage does not simply consist in its fulfilment in Christ. It will also have

GOD

HUMAN BEINGS

Figure 45. The relational dimension: God and human beings

something distinctive to say about God and our relationship with him. God is the hero of the Bible from beginning to end, and he never changes. So we must always ask, 'What does this passage tell me about him?' He is the same God in both the Old Testament and the New: holy, just, loving and sovereign. For example, his deliverance of the Israelites from Egypt not only foreshadows the redemption Christ achieved; it also speaks, in and of itself, of the grace and power of God. We need to let each Old Testament passage speak in its own right before we consider how it points to Christ. It will have something to tell us about God, and it may also have much to say about our relationship with him. Thus Abraham's role in the Bible is not simply to receive the promises Christ fulfilled; he also provides an example of faith for the Christian (Romans 4). And David is not just a model of Christ, the son of David; he is also a model for us as believers in his relationship with God. The Psalms certainly invite us to look forward to Christ, but they also call on us to look up to God and consider our relationship with him. David's experience of the living God challenges us to examine our own. Do we love God and worship him as David did?

That is an appropriate challenge with which to close this book. It will have failed if it leaves its author and readers growing only in intellectual understanding. Let us make sure we do not make the mistake of the Pharisees, who diligently studied the Scriptures and yet refused to come to Jesus to have life (John 5:39–40). As we learn about Christ from the whole Bible, let us determine to love, honour, worship and obey him.

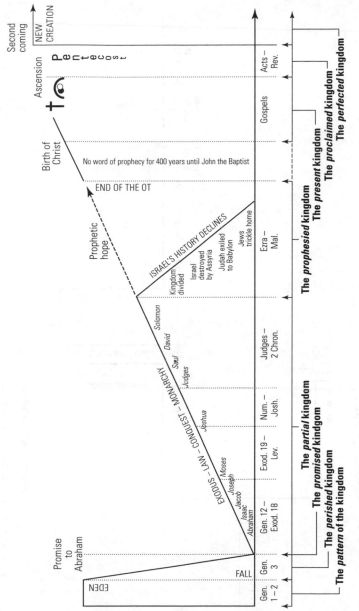

Figure 46. God's big picture

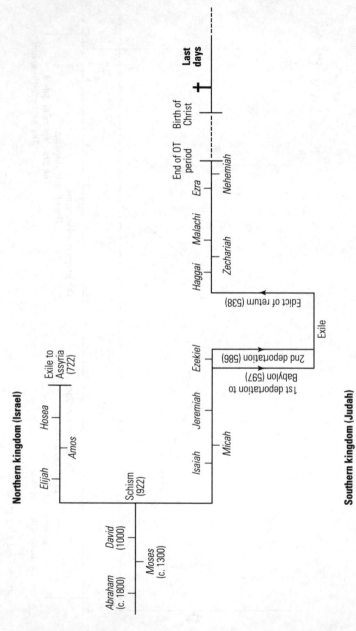

Figure 47. A timeline of Bible history (not to scale)